Favourite Recipes

CW00819677

Geoff Jansz

ALLEN & UNWIN

First published in 1995

Allen & Unwin Pty Ltd
9 Atchison Street
St Leonards NSW 2065, Australia

National Library of Australia
cataloguing-in-publication data

>   Jansz, Geoff, 1958-.
>   Favourite recipes.
>   Includes index.
>   ISBN 1 86448 016 5

>   1. Cookery. I. Title. II: What's cooking
>   (Television program).

>   641.5

Designed by Cornwell Design
Production by MacDux
Cover photography by Bobbi Fabian
Printed by Australian Printing Group, Maryborough, Victoria

10 9 8 7 6 5 4 3 2 1

Contents

Foreword

WE HAVE had great responses to the 'What's Cooking' recipes over the years and *Favourite Recipes* is a collection of those most frequently asked for. Not only are they achievable, they don't cost an arm and a leg.

One of the main areas in which 'What's Cooking' has been very strong is passing on hints and tips. Quite often it's knowing when and how to do the little things that ensures the success of a recipe and this comes from years of experience. Through hosting over 600 shows I have not only *my* ideas to share with you, but also the ideas of the many interesting and successful cooks who have appeared on 'What's Cooking'. This book attempts to carry on the spirit of fun we have in the kitchen while still producing great recipes for your family and friends to share, or just a snack for yourself or the kids. You will find out how to *always* have success with the basics—cooking rice and pasta for example—hints for perfect pickles, pastry, bread, cakes and more, along with tips on storing and selecting the best produce.

I am a great believer in using the freshest seasonal ingredients and in keeping with this, grow my own produce on my farm in the Southern Highlands. Our dynamic Australian food industry is in its most active phase ever: growers are using fewer chemicals and picking fruit and vegetables riper and distributors are delivering supplies in peak condition. We should use this produce in as many different ways as possible. I hope this book reflects the diversity of both our produce and cultural influences—here you will find Thai, Vietnamese, Indian, Italian, French, Greek and Middle-Eastern inspired dishes; new ideas alongside old favourites; dishes to prepare in a hurry as well as meals for special occasions. Above all, the recipes should provide a springboard for your own imagination, and remember, the best food is always provided by cooks who enjoy what they do. Happy Cooking!

Geoff Jansz

Hints & Tips

Apples

> **Apples for cooking:** Golden Delicious apples don't brown as easily as some others do and retain their shape well when cooking. Other apples that hold their shape in cooking are Jonathan and Fuji. When I require a fluffy textured result, I use the 20 Ounce apple or the Granny Smith.

> **Fuji apples** are great to use in salads (see Fuji Apple salad, page 37). A good late variety, in peak season from April to May but available until about September, they are firm, crisp, juicy and their texture is very dense, which means they bruise quite easily, so be careful when handling them. They also store well in the fridge, and don't go floury as easily as some varieties like the Jonathan.

Avocados

> **To ripen avocados:** To speed up the ripening process of an unripe avocado, put it in a brown paper bag with a banana. Store it at room temperature, out of direct sunlight.

Beans

> **To cook beans:** Beans can be prepared in two ways, depending on the amount of time you have. For the traditional long soak method, place the rinsed beans in a bowl with three times as much water and leave overnight. Drain and discard the liquid. Alternatively, put the rinsed beans in a saucepan, cover with water, bring to the boil and boil for 5 minutes. Remove from the heat, cover and set aside for 1½ hours. Drain and discard the liquid.

> Place the prepared beans in a saucepan of water and simmer gently for 30–45 minutes. Drain and discard the liquid.

> Beans should be cooked on the lowest heat (and not bubble) which prevents them from getting battered and breaking up.

Biscuits

> **Rolling biscuit dough:** A sure method of achieving an even thickness to your biscuits is to place two rulers or metal cooking

guides on either side of the dough and resting your rolling pin on them. Roll dough out until it can't be flattened further.

> **Removing biscuits from a tray:** Biscuits are more difficult to remove from a baking tray once they are completely cold. Try using a greased spatula or reheat the tray by running it over a stove burner or briefly returning it to a warm oven.

Blanching

> **To blanch vegetables:** Prepare the vegetables, then drop them into boiling water, wait 30 seconds, then drain and plunge into a bowl of iced water.

> **To intensify the green** of peas and beans, blanch in boiling water for a few seconds, then place immediately in cold water and watch the colour intensify.

Bread

> **Fresh yeast:** This should be more like putty (soft and pliable) rather than dry and crumbly with a sour smell. Fresh yeast stores well in the freezer.

> Make sure yeast is never mixed with hot liquid—it will kill the yeast and the dough won't rise. Always make sure you use tepid liquid in any yeast recipe.

> During the **final rising stage**, the surface may be slashed or scored. The slashes increase the area of the crust; the earlier slashes are made, the more they will open as the loaf rises.

> When the loaf is placed in a preheated oven, it expands even more during the first 20 minutes, until the yeast dies and the crust forms. **To slow down the crust's formation** and promote the loaf's expansion, make the oven humid during this period by placing a wide dish of hot water on the floor of the oven while it preheats and when the loaf goes into the oven, spray with fresh water.

> To make **home-made pizzas**, why not pop into your local baker and buy some ready-made bread dough; toppings take no time to prepare.

Breadcrumbs

> **To make breadcrumbs:** Crumb stale or unwanted bread by rubbing through a metal sieve or processing in a blender or food processor. Fresh breadcrumbs can be frozen, packed into freezer bags, for up to 1 month.

> **To make dried breadcrumbs:** Spread the processed crumbs out onto a baking tray and bake in a 160°C oven until crisp and golden. Store in an airtight container.

> **To crumb food:** To get a crispier, crumbier coating, after you've crumbed once, coat with egg/melted butter and crumbs a second time.

Buttermilk

> Buttermilk should be used within a few days of opening. Unopened, it may keep for up to 15 days in the refrigerator.

Cakes

> **Avoid opening the oven door** for at least the first three quarters of the baking time, then open it only sparingly to ascertain the final baking time required.

> **Allow the cake to settle** in the pan before turning it onto a wire rack to cool.

> Do not **ice** the cake until it is completely cold.

> **Using fan-forced ovens:** With fan-forced ovens, it's a good idea to reduce the temperature by 10°C as you may find that cakes cook slightly quicker in fan-forced oven.

> If your cake is brown enough on top but not quite ready in the centre, cover the top loosely with foil.

> **Cake is ready when:** it is a light golden colour and starts shrinking away from the sides of the tin; if you gently touch the top of the cake with your fingertips and it is firm to touch; when a skewer gently inserted into the thickest part of the cake comes out clean.

> Do not wrap or **store the cake** in an airtight container until it is completely cool, otherwise condensation will occur and make the cake soggy.

> **Creaming butter:** When creaming butter, if it becomes runny in hot weather (instead of light and fluffy) put the bowl in the fridge and chill until firm, then begin again. Adding the sugar just after the butter breaks up instead of after it is completely beaten is another way to avoid runny butter in hot weather. If using zest, add the zest to the butter while creaming, the beating releases the flavours.

> **Baking scones:** Always handle a scone dough with a very light hand to achieve the best results. Over-kneading or handling results in tough scones.

Capsicums

> **Buying capsicums:** Purchase well-shaped, thick-walled fruit with a glossy, smooth skin. Store in the crisper section of the refrigerator for up to 7 days.

Cauliflower

> **Buying cauliflower:** Choose creamy-white, compact heads which have the florets closed tightly together and bright green leaves. If it has a yellow tinge to it, then it is over-mature, so don't buy.

Chicken

> The flavour of **corn-fed** and **free-range** chicken is superior and although it is a little more expensive, it's worth it.

> **To mince chicken:** If you don't have a mincer, then use a food processor with the metal blade to mince the chicken, or ask your butcher to do it for you.

Chillies

> **Preparing chillies:** When chillies are cut they exude a volatile oil called capsaicin, which can irritate the skin. It's a good idea to cut

hot chillies under cold running water or to wear rubber gloves when handling them.

Chocolate

> **To melt chocolate:** Break the chocolate into pieces and place in a heatproof bowl over gently simmering water or a double saucepan. Stir until smooth, then proceed with the recipe.

> To melt chocolate in a microwave: Place chocolate into a microwave-safe dish, uncovered, and microwave on LOW or DEFROST. Stir every 20 seconds until chocolate has melted.

Chutney

> Always **warm sugar before adding** it to the chutney it dissolves more quickly and doesn't caramelise at the bottom of the pan.

> **To test when chutney is ready**, draw a wooden spoon across the bottom of the pan—if it leaves a clean line, the chutney is ready.

> **Use warm jars**, not hot, otherwise the chutney will continue to cook and produce air bubbles on the inside of the jar. Put the chutney into jars while it is still hot.

Cornmeal

> **Buying and storing cornmeal:** Cornmeal is processed in two ways—either stone-ground or steel-milled. Stone-ground is softer in texture and is superior in flavour and nutrients to steel-milled cornmeal. Stone-ground cornmeal should be kept in the refrigerator, while steel-milled cornmeal can be kept in an airtight container on the pantry shelf.

Croutons

> **To prepare croutons:** Remove crusts from slices of bread and cut into cubes. Place on an oven tray and bake in 180°C oven for 10–15 minutes or until crisp and golden. They can be made in advance and, when cold, stored in an airtight container.

Custard

> **To save curdled custard:** Creme anglaise curdles when the temperature of the mixture goes too high and the eggs scramble rather than thicken smoothly. To tell if a custard is curdled, slip a metal spoon into it and if tiny dots of cooked egg show up on the metal, it has curdled. Save it by immediately whizzing it in the blender and it should smooth out perfectly. If large pieces of egg show up on the spoon, it has overcurdled and you should go back to square one.

Deep-frying

> Generally, **deep-fry at about 170°C**. Light olive oil imparts little flavour into the food and is quite stable to heat and re-use.

> **To deep-fry Asian noodles:** Heat oil in a deep-fryer to about 170°C and cook rice vermicelli or cellophane noodles straight from the packet until crisp and golden brown. Drain on paper towel. If using Chinese egg noodles they will have to be cooked first according to packet instructions and dried thoroughly before being deep-fried.

Eggplant

> Eggplant **flesh discolours fast**—always use a stainless steel knife and don't process until the last minute when cooking with it. If you are stuck with leftover chopped eggplant, rub the surfaces with a little lemon juice, which will help stop discolouration.

> **To salt or not to salt:** If you want a drier effect, say when frying, salting is a good idea. The key is choose a good eggplant in the first place and it shouldn't have any bitterness. Select eggplants with firm glossy skins, heavy for their size and smaller rather than larger.

Eggs

> **To keep cracked eggs:** Cover tightly in plastic wrap and keep in the fridge until required.

Eggwhites

> When **whisking** the whites of eggs, add a pinch of cream of tartar to help stabilise the whites.

> **Never overbeat** eggwhites—they must still have a glossy sheen to them. Use a metal bowl rather than a glass one.

> **How to save overbeaten eggwhites:** When eggwhites are over-beaten, they are no longer smooth—if this happens, add a raw eggwhite and beat again briefly until smooth. Eggwhites are better slightly underbeaten rather than overbeaten when they become difficult to combine smoothly into batter. Rather than lightening a batter, overbeaten eggwhites will thin out and the batter will be speckled with little dots of white.

> **Whisking eggwhites:** The freshest eggwhites are not the best for whisking—with age, the proteins in the whites develop and become thicker, making the whites beat to a greater volume and silkier smoothness than fresh eggwhites. As long as there are no yolks mixed in, the whites will keep in the fridge for quite a long time. You can tell they are no longer good when they become thin and watery.

> You must **use beaten eggwhites immediately**—have everything else ready, don't let them sit.

> **Don't use eggs straight from the fridge**, allow them to warm to room temperature first.

Flaming spirits

> When flaming spirits, use a twisted piece of absorbent kitchen paper to form a long taper. Flaming destroys the alcohol content of the spirit but leaves all the flavour.

Garlic

> **How to prepare garlic:** Garlic is notoriously hard to peel, but there is an easy way of doing it. Remove the cloves and crush them with the thick end of a large knife (held flat). The aroma will be released and you now have a bruised and peeled clove of garlic.

The garlic can then be minced or chopped, or if you want a smooth consistency, after chopping the garlic, add a little salt and mash it. You will end up with a little purée of garlic.

Ginger

> **To store ginger:** Fresh ginger can often go soggy and wrinkled before you get a chance to use the whole root. Well, how is this for a long term storage method—bury it in a pot of clean sand and keep it moistened in the normal course of watering your plants. Dig it up when needed, rinse it, cut off what you need, then put it back in the sand. It does not germinate but remains fresh for months.

> Another idea is to simply store ginger in a small plastic bag in the freezer. It can be grated without having to be defrosted or peeled, but it will be quite mushy, so this method is not suited to recipes which require the ginger to be in strips or slices.

> Another alternative is to peel the ginger and cut it into chunks. Place it in a clean jar and cover with sherry or gin. Keep the jar in the refrigerator and use as required. It will store indefinitely. The added bonus is you have ginger – flavoured sherry or gin to use in Chinese cooking or in whatever recipe you desire.

Grapes

> **To peel grapes:** Most grapes are easy to peel by hand or with a paring knife. However, should they prove stubborn, then dip them into boiling water, count 5 seconds, then drain. The skins should strip off easily.

Honey

> **To handle honey more easily:** Heat the spoon you are using in hot water, the honey just slides off the spoon.

Jams

> **To test jam**, put a spoonful on a saucer. When the jam is cool, the surface should set and crinkle when pushed with your finger.

Make sure you remove the pan from the heat when the test is being carried out.

> **When making jam from fruit which is overripe** or lacking in pectin, add some underripe green apples as they contain good amounts of pectin which assists in setting.

Leeks

> **Preparing leeks:** Chop off the root ends and trim tops, leaving about 5 cm of the green leaves. Remove the coarse outer leaves and wash thoroughly to remove any dirt trapped inside the leaves.

Lemon grass

> **Buying and preparing lemon grass:** can be purchased by the stalk from Asian stores and good fruit and vegetable shops. Wash each stalk thoroughly. Chop off the tough green top section and use the tender part. The top section needn't be wasted though. Mixed with boiling water it makes a delightful lemon-scented tea.

Lemons (see also Limes)

> **Juice:** squeeze at the last minute as flavour is lost if it is allowed to stand.

Limes

> **Store limes in the freezer**, wrapped individually in plastic freezer wrap. One of the advantages, besides keeping longer, is that they are easier to grate when they are frozen.

> **To get maximum juice:** Put the limes in the microwave for 10 seconds on HIGH or roll them on the kitchen bench with the palm of your hand.

Mayonnaise

> **To rescue curdled mayonnaise:** Keep the curdled mixture and begin again with the same basic egg yolks and salt. Beat them until they are very thick and pale and then with the blender or food processor running, slowly ladle the curdled mixture into the new base.

Meat

> **Use tongs to turn** meat so you don't pierce the surface and allow the juices to escape.

> **Tying meats:** Butcher's twine should be used for tying and sewing—string or cotton will tear flesh and pull through; it can also leave hairs on your food and coloured string will stain it.

> **Standing time:** Let meat and chicken rest for a few minutes after cooking so the meat will be perfectly cooked and the juices will have time to be re-absorbed.

Molasses

> Molasses is a thick, black syrup which is a by-product of sugar refining. It is available in cans and jars at supermarkets and health food shops.

Mushrooms

> **Cleaning mushrooms:** Never wash mushrooms, simply wipe with a clean, damp cloth or clean lightly with a pastry brush.

Mussels

> **To clean mussels:** When tapped, a live mussel should snap shut. Discard any that remain open. Under running water, scrub the shells with a soft nail brush. Using a knife, grasp the beard on the side of the mussel and pull down firmly—the beard should come away easily. Clean and remove beards just before cooking.

Nuts

> **To store nuts:** Store pecans and walnuts in airtight containers in the fridge. They are often sold loose in bulk which is not really the best way to store them as they go rancid quickly, leaving them bitter and unpleasant tasting. Walnuts in their shells are more likely to be Australian, while shelled ones are more likely to be Californian. If you buy them unshelled, eat them quickly.

Okra

> There are two varieties of okra, a small one, Tender pod which is no more than 4–5 cm long, and a longer pod, Long Green, about 9–12 cm. An okra any larger than this will be old, fibrous and woody. Choose tender pods that snap easily or burst when lightly pressed. Avoid okra with dull, dry skins. Okra is available in summer and autumn. Store it in the crisper in the refrigerator for up to 4 weeks.

Onions

> **Peeling onions:** If you want to halve or quarter an onion, halve or quarter first then strip off the skin—it will come off much more easily. If you want to use onions whole and peeled, dip them into hot water, then in cold water, the skin should strip off easily.

> **Red onions,** also known as Spanish onions, have a sweet, mild flavour and crisp, purple flesh making them the ideal choice when raw onion is called for in a recipe.

> **To caramelise onions:** Peel two large onions and sweat in 2 tablespoons olive oil. Turn heat down to the lowest setting and cook, covered, for about 40 minutes or until onions are golden brown.

Pancakes and Crepes

> When making pancakes or crepes, why not freeze some for later— lay them between wax paper, freeze and take out when needed. Whip up a filling and have crepes in no time.

Parmesan cheese

> It's best to buy Parmesan cheese in a block and grate it as required. Any leftover grated cheese can be stored in an airtight jar in the refrigerator.

Pastry

> **When making pastry,** the cooler the conditions the better—try to make it before turning on the oven, which heats the kitchen.

Use cool equipment—chill bowls and utensils in the refrigerator. Use iced water.

> **Add the liquid gradually**—too much makes the dough sticky to handle and tough when baked.

> **Chill pastry** dough for 15 minutes in cold weather and 30 minutes in hot weather before rolling out. If the dough has been chilled for a long time, stand it at room temperature until it is soft enough to roll out without cracking.

> **Never turn** a pastry over during rolling.

> **Resting pastry:** To prevent shrinking, roll out the pastry and place it in the pie tin without stretching it. Set the pastry aside for 5 minutes before fluting the edge.

> All dough **keeps well in the fridge** for several days provided it is wrapped in plastic wrap to prevent it from drying out and forming a crust.

> **To blind bake:** Chill the lined pastry tin for about 1 hour to allow the gluten to relax and prevent shrinkage when the pastry is cooked. Cover with kitchen paper (large coffee filters also work well) and fill up to the top with dried beans or rice. Bake at 180°C for 25 minutes. Cool completely.

Pickles and Preserves

> All fruit and vegetables must be **carefully washed**—soil residues can cause mould and with so many fruits and vegetables being frequently sprayed when grown commercially, it is important to wash any residues from the skins. All jars must be sterilised.

> **To sterilise jars:** Wash the jars in hot water and detergent, rinse thoroughly and dry them in an oven at 100–120°C, about 30 minutes.

> For **pickles**, use whole spices; powdered ones will cloud the pickle.

> Completely **cover the contents of the jar with the cooking liquid** before sealing or the uncovered food will perish and result in the whole jar spoiling.

> If you want a very **crisp pickle**, leave the vinegar to get cold before adding it to the jar.

> **Avoid metal lids**—use plastic twist tops with a plastic seal inside.

> **Store in a cool, dry place,** preferably away from the light. Light causes them to darken and become murky after a month or two.

Potatoes

> **Potatoes for mashing or grating:** Try Sebago or Desiree which are good for making hash browns.

> **Potatoes for roasting:** Some good roasting potatoes are Sebago, Pontiac, Desiree, Kipfler, Kennebec, Russet Burbank and Toolangi Delight.

Pumpkin

> **Buying pumpkin:** When buying whole, select the fully mature pumpkins that are nice and heavy for their size and free of blemishes. Make sure that the stalk is still intact—if it is damaged, the pumpkin will begin to rot where the stalk and the fruit meet. If the stalk has been removed, you can drip wax from a candle onto the damaged area until it is completely sealed.

> **Store whole pumpkins** in an airy, cool place and they keep for months. If you buy pumpkin in pieces, remove the seeds and membrane and store in the fridge for about a week.

> For **easy peeling**, boil or bake the pumpkin first and then remove the skin, being careful not to damage the flesh.

> **Butternuts** are ideal for soup because they are sweet and tender.

> **Defrosted pumpkin soup** often separates—blend or beat before reheating to bring it back to a smooth consistency.

> **Using leftover pumpkin soup:** Take the pumpkin soup and thin it out with a little extra stock or water. Place in a frying-pan with 1 sliced onion, 150 g sliced ham, a handful of almond slivers and bring just to the frying point and remove from the pan. Scatter this

mixture over pasta with a handful of freshly chopped parsley and a grinding of black pepper.

Rice (also see Basics)

> When you take your **cooked rice** off the heat, place a tea-towel over the rice under the lid to help keep the rice dry.

> **Arborio rice:** For risotto your first choice should be Italian risotto rice, which is called arborio. If this is unavailable, then try Sunwhite Calrose rice.

Rice paper

> Rice paper is a semi-translucent, edible material made from the pith of the Chinese rice paper tree. It is used to wrap both sweet and savoury food. It is available from Asian shops and good delicatessens.

Salsas

> Salsas don't store well like pickles; they last only a few days at the most.

Sauces

> When **melting butter into a sauce**, keep it moving in the pan to prevent it from separating and becoming oily.

> **Making a roux:** A roux is used to thicken soups and sauces and consists of butter and flour cooked together. The flour is stirred into the melted butter and cooked for 1–2 minutes before the liquid is added.

> **Hoi sin sauce** from Hong Kong is superior. You can buy it from Asian grocery stores.

Sesame seeds

> **To toast sesame seeds:** Place in a non-stick frying-pan and dry-roast them over medium heat until golden brown. Remove from the pan immediately or they may overcook.

Souffles

> A pan of water placed in the oven when cooking a souffle creates steam, which prevents the souffle boiling and helps make it lighter.

Stocks

> Never salt a stock.

> For white stocks, always wash the bones thoroughly under cold water first to remove any blood.

> Add enough cold water to cover the bones completely.

> **Boiling stock**: Never boil a stock unless it has been strained of all solids and you are reducing it.

Strawberries

> To wash strawberries: Always wash strawberries before removing the hulls; water can enter the cavity and dilute the flavour.

Tahini

> Tahini is a paste made from ground sesame seeds, widely used in Middle Eastern food. It is available in jars from health food shops and good delicatessens.

Tomatoes

> **Ripen tomatoes** stem-side down, not touching one another, in a dish at room temperature, out of direct sunlight until they become a bright red colour. Ripe tomatoes can be refrigerated for up to a week.

> It's better to remove tomatoes from the refrigerator one hour before eating to get the **full tomato flavour**.

> When **roasting tomatoes**, if they are not very ripe, or you are trying to use some that have not been vine-ripened, sprinkle some sugar on them before they go into the oven. If you turn the heat down to about 120°C and keep drying the tomatoes until they are

very dry (not juicy in the centre), but not dried out and crispy, then they will store well, immersed in oil as 'sun-dried' tomatoes.

> **Peeling tomatoes:** Dip in boiling water for a minute or two and the skin will peel off easily or use a sharp paring knife and peel.

Vanilla Beans

> To make **vanilla sugar** (good for sprinkling on cakes and desserts) split a vanilla pod, place it in a jar of castor sugar and store in the freezer or fridge.

Vegetables

> If cooking **on the barbecue**, microwave first. The vegetables will be cooked all the way through instead of burnt on the outside and raw inside.

Zucchini

> **Buying zucchini:** Choose firm, smooth-skinned zucchini that have a good shape and are heavy for their size. Store in a plastic bag in the refrigerator.

NOTE: these are Australian measurements where the tablespoon measure is 20 ml. In other countries the tablespoon measure is 15 ml. For small measurements (bicarb, baking powder etc.), add a pinch extra for each tablespoon.

Liquids

Metric	Imperial	Cups
15 ml	1/2 fl oz	1 tablespoon
30 ml	1 fl oz	1/8 cup
60 ml	2 fl oz	1/4 cup
90 ml	3 fl oz	
125 ml	4 fl oz	1/2 cup
150 ml	5 fl oz	
170 ml	5 1/2 fl oz	
180 ml	6 fl oz	3/4 cup
220 ml	7 fl oz	
250 ml	8 fl oz	1 cup
500 ml	16 fl oz	2 cups
600 ml	20 fl oz	2 1/2 cups

Dry ingredients

Metric	Imperial	Metric	Imperial
15 g	1/2 oz	315 g	10 oz
30 g	1 oz	345 g	11 oz
60 g	1 oz	375 g	12 oz (3/4 lb)
90 g	3 oz	410 g	13 oz
125 g	4 oz (1/4 lb)	440 g	14 oz
155 g	5 oz	470 g	15 oz
185 g	6 oz	500 g	16 oz (1 lb)
220 g	7 oz	750 g	24 oz (1 1/2 lb)
250 g	8 oz (1/2 lb)	1 kg	32 oz (2 lb)
280 g	9 oz		

Oven temperatures

Temps	Celsius	Fahrenheit	Gas mark
Very Slow	120	250	1/2
Slow	150	300	2
Moderately Slow	160–180	325–350	3–4
Moderate	190–200	375–400	5–6
Moderately hot	220–230	425–450	7
Hot	250–260	475–500	8–9

Cake tin sizes

Round	Square	Springform
20 cm–8 inches	12.5 cm–5 inches	24 cm–9 1/2 inches
22.5 cm–9 inches	20 cm–8 inches	26 cm–10 1/2 inches
25 cm–10 inches	30 cm–12 inches	28 cm–11 inches

Cups and spoons

Metric cup

1/4 cup	60 ml	2 fl oz
1/3 cup	80 ml	2 1/2 fl oz
1/2 cup	125 ml	4 fl oz
1 cup	250 ml	8 fl oz

Metric spoon

1/4 teaspoon	1.25 ml
1/2 teaspoon	2.5 ml
1 teaspoon	5 ml
1 tablespoon	20 ml

Soups

Hungarian mushroom soup with a puff pastry cap

IT'S RICH mushroom flavour and melt-in-the-mouth pastry makes this impressive dish ideal for entertaining.

Some good mushroom varieties available in supermarkets are Swiss brown, Roman brown and shiitake. They are all meaty and flavoursome; try them as an alternative to the usual mushies.

Serves 6

2 medium-size onions, chopped
2 cloves garlic, chopped
1 1/2 tablespoons Hungarian paprika
100 g butter
3 tablespoons flour
500 g fresh mushrooms (use a variety if you wish), sliced ☞
3 cups chicken stock
1 1/2 cups milk
1 teaspoon salt
freshly ground black pepper to taste
1 tablespoon lemon juice
1 cup sour cream
1/3 cup chopped fresh parsley and/or fresh dill
ready-rolled puff pastry
beaten egg for glazing

In a large saucepan, sauté the onions, garlic and paprika in half the butter for a few minutes to soften. Add flour and continue cooking for about 3 minutes or until the flour is cooked. Remove from the pan.

Melt the remaining butter in the pan, add the mushrooms and sweat for about 10 minutes until they have softened. Return the flour and onion mixture to the pan and stir in the chicken stock and milk. Season with salt and pepper and simmer for 10 minutes.

Stir in the lemon juice, sour cream and parsley and leave to cool.

Cut squares of pastry big enough to cover some deep bowls. Spoon the soup into the bowls and brush the rims with beaten egg. Top each bowl with pastry and press down to seal the pastry to the rim. Trim away the excess with a sharp knife, brush the pastry with beaten egg and top with a mushroom shape, cut from a scrap of pastry.

Place bowls of soup on a baking tray and bake in a 200°C oven for about 20–30 minutes or until the pastry is puffed and golden brown. Take to the table and serve straight away.

☞ *Hint: See Cleaning Mushrooms, page 11*

Roasted tomato soup

ROASTING THE tomatoes and capsicums concentrates and caramelises them and gives this soup a wonderfully rich, full-bodied flavour. It makes a great weekend luncheon dish served with crusty bread.

Serves 4–6

    1 kg large, firm but ripe tomatoes ☞
    olive oil
    salt and freshly ground black pepper to taste
    3 red capsicums
    2 tablespoons butter or olive oil
    1 small carrot, chopped
    1 onion, chopped
    2 cloves garlic
    2 cups chicken stock
    ½ cup pure cream

Preheat the oven to 220°C. Cut the tomatoes in half and squeeze out the seeds. Toss them with olive oil and season to taste with salt and pepper. Place on a baking tray, cut-side down. Grill until the skins blister and puff up, then remove the skins and turn them over. Bake in preheated oven with the capsicums for 30 minutes. Cool, then skin and seed capsicums, reserving flesh and juices.

Melt the butter in a medium-size saucepan and sauté the carrot, onion and garlic without colouring until they are soft. Add the stock and season with salt and pepper, then simmer for 30 minutes. Add the tomato and capsicum flesh and the juices, then purée or sieve the soup. Correct the seasoning and add the cream. Heat through but do not boil again.

☞ *Hint: See Ripen Tomatoes, page 16*

French onion soup

THE SEGMENT Old Favourites is always popular on 'What's Cooking'. This was our most popular old favourite in Soup week during winter 1994.

Serves 6

   125 g butter
   6 large onions, sliced
   1 tablespoon flour
   4 cups strong beef stock
   1/3 cup white wine
   salt and freshly ground black pepper to taste
   1 tablespoon Cognac
   2 tablespoons chopped fresh parsley
   a dash of red wine vinegar
   French bread stick, sliced and toasted
   Gruyere cheese, grated

Melt the butter in a large, heavy-based saucepan over a medium heat and sauté the onion for 20–25 minutes or until browned, stirring occasionally. Add the flour and stir for a few minutes.

Add the stock and wine and bring to the boil. Season to taste with salt and pepper.

Simmer for about 20 minutes, then stir in the Cognac and parsley and vinegar to taste.

Ladle into soup bowls and top with a piece of toasted French stick and some grated Gruyere cheese. Place the bowls under the griller until the cheese melts, then serve.

☞ *Hint: See Boiling Stock, page 16*

Quick curried cauliflower soup

THIS IS an example of how easily available ingredients combine in a simple way to quickly produce a delicious meal. Flicking through this book in search of a meal idea, it would be understandable to pass over this recipe thinking it appeared too simple or unexciting. Please give it a go—you'll be surprised. There's the added bonus of costing practically nothing.

Serves 4

- 1/2 small cauliflower ☞
- 1 tablespoon butter or oil
- 1 onion, chopped
- 2 teaspoons curry powder
- 2 cups chicken stock or water
- 1/2 cup cream (optional)

Chop the cauliflower into small pieces. Heat the butter in a large saucepan and cook the onion and curry powder over medium heat for about 15 minutes. Add the cauliflower and stock. Simmer until tender, then purée .

Add cream to thicken if desired.

☞ *Hint: Buying Cauliflower, page 5*

Chervil soup

CHERVIL is quite a delicate herb and its fine fern-like appearance
has made it a popular garnish. Its flavour is milder than parsley and is
slightly anise. This is a very basic soup method and other herbs can
be substituted. But add them to taste— two handfuls of sage, for
instance, would be far too powerful.

Serves 6

    2 tablespoons butter
    2 tablespoons flour
    4 cups chicken stock
    1/4 cup cream
    salt and freshly ground black pepper to taste
    2 handfuls fresh chervil, chopped

In a saucepan, melt the butter and add the flour. Cook over medium
heat for 2 minutes, stirring constantly. Stir in the stock and bring to
the boil. Simmer for 5 minutes, then add cream and season to taste
with salt and pepper.

Throw in the chopped chervil and serve at once.

☞ *Hint: See Sauces, Making A Roux, page 15*

Gazpacho

SOMETIMES described as a soup–salad, this colourful Spanish dish makes a refreshing summer meal. Look out for the raw garlic – it lingers, but it's worth it. Making the Gazpacho in a food processor is not traditional and turns the tomato a paler colour.

1 kg ripe red tomatoes, peeled ☞
2 cloves garlic, crushed
1 red onion, chopped
150 g green capsicum, chopped
150 g continental cucumber, seeded
1 teaspoon salt
freshly ground black pepper to taste
1/2 cup Spanish olive oil
100 ml sherry vinegar
100 g crustless white bread, soaked in water, then drained
water—up to 2 cups
2 cups tomato juice
1/4 cup tomato paste
pinch of ground cumin
pinch of cayenne or some Tabasco sauce to taste

Place the tomatoes, garlic, onion, capsicum and cucumber in a bowl. Add the salt, pepper, oil and vinegar, toss well and leave to marinate for an hour or so.

Place all the vegetables in a blender or food processor with the soaked bread and the water (the amount of water will depend on your taste) and blend until the consistency is as you like it.

Blend in the tomato juice and paste and season to taste with the cumin and cayenne. Leave to stand overnight if time permits.
Serve with chopped boiled egg, garlic croutons, chopped capsicums, chopped onion and chopped olives.

Gazpacho must be served icy cold and must therefore be very well seasoned. Thin with iced water if necessary.

Pumpkin Soup

I LIKE this soup—it's simple and effective because it tastes like pumpkin. I've seen too many recipes that include all manner of ingredients which end up masking the flavour of the pumpkin.

Use a hollowed out golden nugget pumpkin as an attractive serving bowl.

Serves 6

> 200 g butter
> 4 cups pumpkin, peeled and cut into 2 cm cubes
> 1 onion, chopped
> 2 cups chicken stock
> salt and freshly ground black pepper to taste
> croutons
> sour cream
> chives

Melt the butter in a saucepan and slowly sweat the pumpkin and onion, cover with a lid, stirring occasionally, until quite tender.

Blend the pumpkin in a food processor until it is quite smooth. Return to the saucepan and mix in the chicken stock. Pumpkins vary in moisture content, so if you need to, adjust the thickness of the soup with the chicken stock.

Season to taste with salt and pepper. Serve with croutons, sour cream, and chopped chives.

☞ *Hint: See Using Leftover Pumpkin Soup, page 14*

Thai-style prawn soup with basil

Thai basil is green-leafed with purple stems and has a unique and slightly aniseed flavour

Serves 4–6

    250 g green prawns
    1 tablespoon oil
    400 ml coconut cream
    2 cups boiling water
    2 cloves garlic, crushed
    2 teaspoons grated ginger ☞
    4 spring onions, chopped
    2 small fresh red chillies, chopped
    1 tablespoon chopped fresh lemon grass
    500 g pumpkin, cubed
    3 tablespoons fish sauce
    1 tablespoon brown sugar
    1/4 cup fresh Thai or sweet basil leaves

Shell and de-vein the prawns, reserving the heads and shells. Set the prawns aside and fry the heads and shells in a little of the oil in a medium-size saucepan until they turn pink and aromatic. Add the coconut cream and water and simmer for 20–30 minutes, then strain. Discard the shells and set the stock aside.

Heat the remaining oil in a saucepan, add the garlic, ginger, spring onions, chillies and lemon grass. Cook, stirring, until the spring onions have softened. Add the pumpkin. Add the prawn stock and bring to the boil. Simmer, covered, for 15 minutes until the pumpkin is tender. Add the fish sauce, brown sugar and the prawns. Bring to a simmer, then remove from the heat—the prawns will cook in the residual heat of the soup. Stir in the basil leaves and serve.

☞ Hint: See To Store Ginger, page 9

Salads

Vietnamese-style chicken salad

VIETNAMESE cooking is becoming extremely popular these days, which isn't surprising because it combines fresh ingredients with tangy herbs and spices to form mouth-watering meals that don't bulge the waistline.

Asian greens are now readily available and easy to grow. I grow a lot of bok choy, which would work well with this recipe, as would choi sum, which has softer, finer stems and more green leaf.

Serves 2

- 2 stalks lemon grass, (only tender part) roughly chopped ☞
- 2 cloves garlic, peeled
- 2 tablespoons fish sauce
- freshly ground black pepper to taste
- 2 chicken thigh fillets
- 2 tablespoons peanut oil
- 1–2 small red chillies, split and seeded
- 4 spring onions, cut into 2 cm pieces
- 2 tablespoons roasted peanuts, chopped
- 2 teaspoons sugar
- 1 tablespoon white vinegar
- Asian greens
- 1/2 cup fresh mint leaves
- 1/2 cup fresh coriander leaves
- 5 cm piece of carrot, cut into very fine strips
- 1 medium-size Lebanese cucumber, cut into fine strips
- a little rice vermicelli, soaked in boiling water (optional)
- 2 tablespoons deep-fried shallots (available from Asian food stores)
- extra coriander leaves for garnish

Combine the lemon grass, garlic, fish sauce and pepper in a food processor and process until quite fine. Coat the chicken with the mixture and allow to stand for about an hour. Drain the chicken, reserving the marinade, and barbecue or pan-fry over high heat on both sides until cooked.

Heat the peanut oil in a wok and quickly stir-fry the chilli, spring onions and peanuts, then add the reserved marinade. Season to taste with sugar and vinegar.

Arrange the greens, mint, coriander, carrot and cucumber on a plate and place the drained vermicelli to one side. Slice the chicken and arrange over the greens. Pour over the dressing and sprinkle with deep-fried shallots and extra coriander leaves.

☞ *Hint: See Buying and Preparing Lemon Grass, page 10*

Chicken Waldorf salad

THE ADDITION of tender chicken to this classic salad transforms an old favourite into a quick and satisfying meal.

Serves 4

2–3 chicken fillets
salt and freshly ground black pepper to taste
4 sticks celery, cut into bite-size pieces
2 apples, red or green, peeled if you like
½ cup walnuts or pecans, lightly roasted ☞
cos lettuce leaves, washed and dried
extra walnuts to garnish
fresh herbs to sprinkle

Mayonnaise ☞

2 egg yolks
1½ tablespoons red or white vinegar
salt and freshly ground white pepper to taste
1–2 tablespoons Dijon mustard
1½ cups light olive oil

Cut the chicken fillets into broad strips and flatten slightly with a mallet. Sauté the strips in a little oil on a grill plate, barbecue or in a frying-pan, then season with salt and pepper.

To make the mayonnaise: Drop the egg yolks into a bowl and using a whisk or electric beater, mix in the vinegar, salt, pepper and mustard. Beating continuously, add the oil in a thin stream (very slowly at first or it may curdle).

Place the celery in a bowl with the apple and nuts. Dress with about ¾ cup of mayonnaise (store the rest in a glass jar in the fridge). Place cos lettuce on serving plates. Top with the Waldorf salad, then the chicken strips. Sprinkle walnuts and fresh herbs over the top.

☞ Hint: See To Rescue Curdled Mayonnaise, page 10, and To Store Nuts, page 11

Warm chilli egg salad

THIS SIMPLE dish is surprisingly tasty and perfect for a quick lunch or summer supper dish.

Serves 4

   5 eggs, hard-boiled and shelled
   1/2 cup egg mayonnaise ☞
   1/3 cup light sour cream
   1 teaspoon Tabasco or other chilli sauce (or to taste)
   2 tablespoons chopped fresh parsley or coriander

Chop the eggs and mix with the mayonnaise, sour cream, Tabasco and parsley. If the eggs were cold, it's quite nice to warm this dish up a bit in the microwave.

Serve with bread and lettuce.

☞ *Hint: See Basics Mayonnaise, page 157*

Red salad

THIS SALAD has a crunchy texture and delicious flavour. Its ruby colour gives it a festive look, so serve it as part of a summer buffet.

Serves 6–8

  2 medium-size raw beetroot, peeled and grated
  1/2 red cabbage, finely shredded
  1 large red onion, finely sliced ☞
  2 Red Delicious apples, cored and cut into cubes

Dressing

  1 tablespoon red wine vinegar
  1/4 cup olive oil
  2 tablespoons apple juice concentrate (or 1 tablespoon honey)
  salt and freshly ground black pepper to taste

Combine beetroot, cabbage, onion and apple in a large salad bowl.

To prepare the dressing: Combine all ingredients well. Pour over salad and toss well. Serve immediately.

☞ Hint: See Red Onions, page 12

Fuji apple salad

I GROW Fujis on my farm at Bowral. They are a late variety—in peak season from April to May, although you can get them through to September. They are firm, crisp, juicy apples with a dense texture—which means they bruise easily.

3 Fuji apples, cored and sliced
juice of half lemon ☞
150 g snow peas, blanched
1 cos or other lettuce
6 rashers bacon, crisply grilled

Dressing
1/2 cup mayonnaise (home-made is best, see Basics, page 157)
1/4 cup apple juice
1/3 cup pecan nuts
1 shallot, peeled

Place the apples and lemon juice in a bowl and toss to coat.
Add the snow peas and lettuce leaves.

To prepare dressing: Place the dressing ingredients in a food processor and blend until the nuts are fine. Pour over the salad ingredients and toss to coat. Place in an edible salad bowl (see choux pastry edible salad bowl, page 152) and crumble the bacon over the top.

☞ Hint: See Lemon Juice, page 10

Tabouli

The flat leafed continental parsley is far more flavoursome and it's also very easy to grow which makes tabouli a real option for the home gardener.

Serves 4–6

  2/3 cup burghul (steamed cracked wheat)
  2 cups chopped continental parsley
  1/2 cup shredded mint
  3 tablespoons thinly sliced spring onions
  1/4 cup olive oil
  1/4 cup lemon juice
  1 vine-ripened tomato or 1/2 cup cherry tomatoes, diced
  salt and freshly ground black pepper to taste

Soak the burghul in enough water to cover for at least 30 minutes. Place in a sieve to drain, then press out excess water.

Place burghul in a bowl and add remaining ingredients.
Toss together and serve after 10 minutes.

Quick Meals & Snacks

Felafel

THE OIL temperature is important here—the colour of the felafels must be perfectly brown by the time they are cooked through. Just under the temperature for cooking chips is best for felafels the size of a dessertspoon, around 160°C.

Serves 4

> 4 slices brown bread
> 375 g can chickpeas (or 1 cup chickpeas, soaked overnight in 3 cups water)
> 1/4 cup pinenuts
> 2 cloves garlic, crushed
> 1/4 cup chopped fresh parsley
> 1/4 cup self-raising flour
> 1 tablespoon lemon juice
> 1 tablespoon tahini ☞
> 1 teaspoon ground cumin
> 1 tablespoon chopped fresh coriander
> 1 small fresh red chilli, finely chopped (or 1/4 teaspoon chilli powder)
> salt and freshly ground black pepper to taste
> oil for deep-frying

Yoghurt sauce

> 1 cup thick natural yoghurt
> 1 clove garlic, crushed
> 1 teaspoon finely chopped mint
> 1 tablespoon tahini

Soak the bread in water, then squeeze dry. Place soaked chickpeas, bread, pinenuts, garlic and parsley in a food processor and process to a coarse paste. Blend in the flour, lemon juice, tahini, cumin, coriander, chilli and salt and pepper.

Moisten your hands and shape the mixture into walnut-sized balls. Refrigerate for 30 minutes.

Heat sufficient oil to deep-fry the felafel. Deep-fry 6 or 7 at a time in the hot oil for approximately 5 minutes or until golden brown. Drain on paper towels.

To prepare the yoghurt sauce: Combine all ingredients. Refrigerate until required

Serve felafels with yoghurt sauce, salad and pita bread.

☞ *Hint: See Tahini, page 16*

Pan-cooked Tex-Mex pizza

FOR THOSE with a fear of yeast cookery, here is a pizza base with
some lift but without the 3 or 4 stages required to make conventional
pizzas.

Makes 1 large family-size pizza

Base

1 cup plain flour
1 teaspoon baking powder
pinch of salt
about 1/2 cup water
a little olive oil

Spicy Mexican bean topping

440 g can borlotti beans or red kidney beans, rinsed and drained
2 tablespoons olive oil
1 clove garlic, chopped
1 small onion, chopped
1/4 teaspoon paprika
1/2 teaspoon ground cumin
1/4 teaspoon chilli powder or cayenne (or to taste)
1/4 teaspoon freshly ground black pepper
2 teaspoons tomato paste
2 teaspoons sugar
1/2 teaspoon salt
1/2 cup corn kernels
1/2 green capsicum, chopped
mozzarella cheese, sliced or grated
sour cream to serve

To prepare the base: Place the flour, baking powder and salt in a bowl. Add enough water to make a soft dough. Knead for a couple of minutes, then roll into a ball. Allow to rest for a few more minutes, then roll out to form a disc large enough to fit in your frying-pan.

Brush the frying-pan with the oil and lift the dough onto it. Neaten the edges, then cook over high heat for about 3 minutes. Reduce the heat and cook for another 2 minutes or until the base has browned and the dough is cooked.

Cover with Spicy Mexican Bean Topping or the toppings of your choice and place under a hot griller for about 5 minutes or until the topping is cooked.

To prepare the Spicy Mexican Bean Topping: Mash half the beans (or purée them in a food processor).

Heat the oil in a frying-pan over a medium heat and cook the garlic, onion and spices for 2–3 minutes.

Add the mashed beans, tomato paste, sugar and salt and stir over a medium heat for a few minutes.

Spoon the bean mixture onto the pizza base, then top with some corn kernels, green capsicum and mozzarella cheese. Cook under the griller until the cheese is lightly browned. Serve topped with sour cream.

☞ *Hint: See To Make Home-made Pizzas, page 3*

Boston-style baked beans

THIS RECIPE is equally nice without bacon bones. Simply use water or vegetable stock for a vegetarian alternative. These baked beans will keep up to three days in the refrigerator and their flavour will improve with reheating. They also freeze extremely well in small batches.

Serves 6

> 500 g haricot beans (navy beans) or canellini beans
> 1 tablespoon olive oil
> 2 onions, diced
> 450 g bacon bones
> 500 ml water
> 140 g tub tomato paste
> 1 tablespoon French mustard
> 1 tablespoon brown sugar
> 1 tablespoon molasses ☞
> 1 tablespoon Worcestershire sauce
> salt and freshly ground black pepper to taste

The beans can be prepared in two ways, depending on the amount of time you have.

For the traditional long soak method, place the rinsed beans in a bowl with three times as much water and leave overnight. Drain and discard the liquid.

Alternatively, put the rinsed beans in a saucepan, cover with water, bring to the boil and boil for 5 minutes. Remove from the heat, cover and set aside for 1 1/2 hours. Drain and discard the liquid.

Place the prepared beans in a saucepan full of water and simmer gently for 30–45 minutes. Drain and discard the liquid. (Canned beans can be substituted at this point if desired)

Heat the oil in a pan and sauté the onion until softened.

Place the bacon bones and water in a large saucepan and simmer for 40 minutes. Remove the bones and add the stock to the beans. Trim the meat from the bones. Discard bones and chop meat finely. Add meat to the stock and beans with the remaining ingredients. Simmer for 20–30 minutes until the mixture thickens and beans soften. Season to taste.

Serve with hot buttered toast.

☞ *Hint: See Molasses, page 11*

Polenta chips

THIS IS a classic case of modern appliances stepping in to assist with previously laborious cooking steps—making polenta. One of our 'What's Cooking' team, Phil Neil, taught me this.

Makes one large bowl

> 1 1/2 cups polenta
> 6 cups water
> 50 g Parmesan cheese, finely grated
> 100 g mozzarella cheese, cut into cubes
> 1 1/2 teaspoons salt
> freshly ground black pepper to taste
> flour for coating
> 2 eggs, lightly beaten
> 2 cups fresh breadcrumbs
> oil for deep-frying

Place the polenta in a large microwave-safe bowl or casserole dish and whisk in the water. Cover and cook on HIGH for 6 minutes. Stir, re-cover and cook for a further 6 minutes.

Allow to stand for 5 minutes to allow the polenta to thicken and firm.

Add the cheeses, salt and pepper and press into an oiled baking tray. Allow to cool until completely cold and set.

Cut into fingers and toss gently in the flour. Dip the floured fingers in beaten egg, drain, then roll in the breadcrumbs. Refrigerate for 30 minutes.

Heat the oil in a large frying-pan. Shake excess coating off chips and deep-fry until golden brown. Drain well on paper towel, then serve with a Tomato Sauce, for recipe, see Basics chapter page 156.

☞ Hint: See Deep-frying, page 7

Parsi omelette

A CLASSIC Indian regional dish.

Serves 2

　　30 g butter or oil
　　1 medium-size onion, finely chopped
　　5 eggs ☞
　　2 tablespoons chopped fresh coriander leaves
　　1 small red chilli, seeded and chopped
　　1 clove garlic, crushed
　　1 teaspoon grated fresh ginger
　　salt and freshly ground black pepper to taste
　　2 tablespoons tamarind purée (available at good
　　　　delicatessens, or use the juice and zest of 1 lemon)

Heat the butter in a non-stick frying-pan and fry the onion until pale gold.

Beat the eggs in a bowl and stir in coriander, chilli, garlic, ginger, salt, pepper and tamarind purée. Pour the egg mixture over the onions in the pan, stir mixture and cook until the bottom is set. Finish off under a hot griller, then serve at once with salad.

☞ *Hint: See To Keep Cracked Eggs, page 7*

Pumpkin pancake stack

This recipe is popular because of its appeal to children—most love pancakes. So when Mum and Dad are struggling to make the little ones eat vegies, use a little psychology and a lot of camouflage.

Serves 4–6

Pancakes

1 ½ cups cooked pumpkin flesh (700 g uncooked)
1 ½ cups self-raising flour
2 eggs
salt and freshly ground black pepper to taste
freshly grated nutmeg
¾ cup milk

Filling

1 cob corn
½ red capsicum, finely diced
½ green capsicum, finely diced
1 onion, chopped
1 tablespoon olive oil
salt and freshly ground black pepper to taste
pinch of paprika
200 ml light sour cream
grated Cheddar cheese (optional)

To prepare the pancakes: Place the pumpkin in a mixing bowl and mix in the flour and eggs. Season with salt, pepper and nutmeg and add enough milk to bring to a pouring consistency.

Pour ¾ cup of the mixture into an oiled, non-stick frying-pan and cook over a medium heat until golden on either side. Remove and rest on paper towels, keep warm. Continue until the mixture is used.

To prepare the filling: Blanch the corn in boiling water, or in the microwave, until tender, then set aside.

Place the remaining vegetables in a pan with the olive oil and cook gently until they are tender. Season with salt, pepper and paprika.

Cut the kernels from the corn cob using a sharp knife and add to the pan with the sour cream.

Preheat the oven to 200°C. Layer the pancakes in a baking dish with the vegetable filling and top with grated cheese if desired.

Bake in the oven for about 15 minutes or until the cheese is melted and golden brown.

☞ *Hint: See Pancakes and Crepes, page 12*

Hash pinks

THIS DELIGHTFUL variation of an old favourite is delicious served with barbecued meats.

Serves 4

  2 floury potatoes ☞
  1 medium-size beetroot
  salt and freshly ground black pepper to taste
  olive oil

Grate the potatoes and the beetroot. Squeeze out the excess juice and season with salt and pepper.

Heat a little olive oil in a frying-pan and add the grated vegetables. Flatten out into a large pancake and cook on one side until crispy. Invert onto a baking tray and slip back into the pan to cook the second side.

Serve as a side dish with barbecued meats or with scrambled eggs and crisply grilled bacon.

☞ *Hint: See Potatoes, page 14*

Bombay chicken wings

A GREAT little pre-dinner snack.

Serves 8

1 kg chicken wings
1/2 cup natural yoghurt
1/2 teaspoon salt
1/2 teaspoon turmeric
1-2 cloves garlic, crushed
2 teaspoons finely grated ginger
1 teaspoon freshly ground black pepper
1/2 teaspoon chilli powder
1 teaspoon garam marsala
2 teaspoons paprika
2 tablespoons oil
juice of half a lemon
1 teaspoon cumin seeds

Cut the chicken wings into separate digits. Reserve the wing tips for stock. Chop the knuckle from the other end of each wing digit and pull the meat down to one end of the bone. Repeat this process with each wing. (Some of the digits have two bones—remove the small one.) Place all the wings in a bowl.

Mix together the yoghurt, salt, turmeric, garlic, ginger, pepper, chilli powder, garam marsala, paprika, oil and lemon juice and toss through the wings. Allow to stand for two hours or refrigerate overnight.

Place the wings on a rack in a baking dish, sprinkle with cumin seeds and cook in a 250°C oven for about 15–20 minutes. Serve hot.

☞ Hint: See Standing Time, page 11

Smoked trout with leeks on little pikelets

SMOKED trout is not expensive and is perfect for an hors d'oeuvre because it's smoky, salty and more-ish—great with a drink. Nowadays we're starting to see fresh crabmeat becoming available in vacuum sealed bags—it's usually blue swimmer crab or spanner crab. If you can find this, try it. It's a little more expensive but a small amount goes a long way.

1 smoked trout, or packet of crabmeat
2 tablespoons olive oil
2 leeks, cut into strips, then well washed ☞
2 tablespoons dry white wine or a dash of white vinegar
salt and freshly ground black pepper to taste

Pikelet batter

1 cup self-raising flour
pinch of salt
1 tablespoon castor sugar
1 egg, beaten
1/2 cup milk
1 tablespoon butter

Skin the smoked trout and gently remove the fillets. Break into large, natural flakes.

Heat the oil in a pan and cook the leek until quite soft but not brown. Add the white wine, season well with salt and pepper and allow to reduce.

Place a spoonful of leek onto each pikelet and top with a small piece of smoked trout or crabmeat. Arrange on a serving platter and serve warm or cold.

To prepare the pikelet batter: In a large bowl, combine the flour, salt and sugar. Make a well in the centre. Mix the egg and milk together and pour into the flour. Mix with a knife into a smooth batter.

Heat a little butter in a frying-pan. Drop spoonfuls of the pikelet batter into the pan, leaving room for spreading. When bubbles appear on the surface, turn the pikelets over to cook the other side. Keep warm while preparing remaining pikelets.

☞ *Hint: See Preparing Leeks, page 10*

Southern fried chicken burger

THESE ARE especially popular with children as they tend to prefer milder flavours.

Makes 4 burgers

1 medium-size eggwhite ☞
3 tablespoons buttermilk
1 small clove garlic, minced
salt and freshly ground black pepper to taste
1 1/2 cups dry breadcrumbs
600 g chicken breast meat, coarsely minced
1 cup peanut oil
2 tablespoons honey
4 tablespoons seeded mustard
1/2 cup egg mayonnaise
8 slices cornbread or your choice of bread
8 lettuce leaves, washed and dried
4 slices ripe tomato

Whisk together the eggwhite, buttermilk, garlic, salt and pepper. Add this mixture and 1/2 cup of the breadcrumbs to the minced chicken meat. Combine these ingredients gently but thoroughly.

Divide the chicken into four large burgers and lightly coat with the remaining breadcrumbs. Heat the oil in a large frying-pan and cook the burgers on both sides for one minute. Place on a large baking tray and cook in a 180°C oven for approximately 15 minutes.

Mix the honey and mustard with the mayonnaise and spread this over the top and bottom slices of the cornbread. Place a burger on the bottom half, top with lettuce and tomato and close the burger. Serve with a side salad of toasted peanuts and sweetcorn.

☞ Hint: See Whisking Eggwhites, page 8

Pasta & Rice

Radicchio and artichoke risotto

I FIND risotto is a wonderful vehicle for carrying other flavours.

The richness of this risotto is beautifully balanced by the sharpness of the radicchio, which also adds a dash of colour to an otherwise pale dish.

Serves 4–6

- 1 large head radicchio
- 6 preserved artichoke hearts
- 6 tablespoons butter
- 1 large onion, finely chopped
- 4 cloves garlic, finely chopped
- 4 cups chicken stock
- 1 cup Arborio rice ☞
- 3/4 cup freshly grated Parmesan cheese
- salt and freshly ground black pepper to taste
- fresh radicchio leaves 4-6 (optional)
- 1/4 cup finely chopped fresh parsley

Trim the radicchio and cut into quarters. Remove the core and cut the quarters into ribbons. Slice the artichoke hearts.

Heat the butter in a large saucepan and add the radicchio. Sweat for a few minutes until wilted. Remove the radicchio from the pan, leaving the butter behind. Add the onion and garlic to the pan and sauté over medium heat. Meanwhile, bring the stock to a simmer.

Add the rice to the onions and cook for a few minutes. Stir in the stock, a ladleful at a time, stirring until the liquid is absorbed. When the rice is done, about 15 minutes, add the radicchio and the sliced artichokes. Stir in half the cheese and season to taste with salt and pepper. Spoon into a raw radicchio leaf cup, top with the remaining cheese and sprinkle with parsley. Serve.

☞ *Hint: Arborio rice, page 15*

Rice paper rolls

THIS TRADITIONAL Vietnamese dish has a lot going for it—tasty, healthy, portable and easily varied.

Makes 20

  100 g bean shoots
  100 g rice vermicelli
  20 sheets rice paper ☞
  10 cooked prawns
  1 tablespoon shredded mint leaves
  1 tablespoon shredded coriander leaves
  100 g cold roast pork

Dipping sauce

  $1/4$ cup water
  2 tablespoons sugar
  1 tablespoon lemon juice or vinegar
  2 tablespoons fish sauce
  crushed garlic (optional)
  $1/2$ teaspoon pickled red chilli, ground
  1 tablespoon roasted peanuts, ground

Blanch the bean shoots quickly in boiling water, then plunge into cold water. Drain well. Soak the vermicelli in boiling water for 2 minutes, then drain well. Soak the rice paper in warm water for 20 seconds and place on a clean tea-towel to absorb the excess moisture. Split the prawns and remove the vein.

Place some noodles, bean shoots, mint and coriander on a piece of rice paper and roll the rice paper just enough to cover the filling. Tuck in the ends, then place a piece of prawn and some shredded pork in the roll and continue rolling

To prepare the dipping sauce: Boil the water and sugar together for 2 minutes, then allow to cool. Mix in the lemon juice, fish sauce, crushed garlic, pickled red chilli and nuts and serve with the rolls.

☞ Hint: See Rice Paper, page 15

Tortellini with coconut avocado cream

I AM GRADUALLY discovering how to use the microwave for quick and easy home cooking—here is an example, popular with the discerning film crew. This recipe uses shallots, often confused with spring onions. They are cousins, but are quite different. Shallots grow in a cluster of bulbs, similar to garlic, but are covered with a reddish-brown skin. They have a subtle, sweet flavour.

Serves 4

3 rashers bacon, chopped
6 shallots
crushed garlic
500 g fresh tortellini
2 ripe avocados
1/3 cup coconut cream
1 tablespoon lemon juice
salt and freshly ground black pepper to taste
Tabasco sauce to taste
425 g can peeled tomatoes, drained and chopped
1/2 cup grated Parmesan cheese ☞

Place the bacon, shallots and garlic in a small microwave-safe dish. Cook for 4–5 minutes on HIGH.

Place tortellini in a large microwave-safe bowl, cover with hot water, cook for 10–12 minutes on HIGH until tender. Drain.

Blend avocado flesh, coconut cream, lemon juice, salt, pepper and Tabasco sauce until smooth.

Stir in tomatoes, 1/4 cup cheese and bacon mixture. Pour over hot tortellini. Sprinkle with remaining cheese.

Heat for 3–5 minutes on MEDIUM if necessary.

☞ Hint: See Parmesan Cheese, page 12

Lemon risotto with chicken

THIS RECIPE calls for lemon thyme, which has broader leaves than regular thyme and a definite lemon aroma.

Serves 10

30 g butter
2 tablespoons olive oil
1 medium-size onion, finely chopped
2 cups arborio rice
6 cups chicken stock, simmering
100 g Parmesan cheese (in one piece)
15 g extra butter
salt and freshly ground black pepper to taste
1 teaspoon fresh lemon thyme leaves
2 teaspoons chopped fresh sage leaves (or 1 teaspoon dried sage)
1 tablespoon lemon juice
finely grated zest of 1 lemon
fresh young spinach and grilled chicken to accompany

Place the butter and oil in a large saucepan and cook the onion over a medium heat for a few minutes without colouring. Add the rice and fry for a few minutes before ladling in some stock.

Stir the risotto and keep adding a ladleful of simmering stock as it is absorbed by the rice. The rice is cooked when it is still slightly firm to the bite—not completely mushy.

Grate 1/3 of the cheese and stir into the risotto with the extra butter, salt and pepper, herbs and lemon juice and zest.

Serve sprinkled with the remaining grated cheese, accompanied by steamed spinach and grilled chicken.

☞ *Hint: See Stocks, pages 16*

Ricotta pasta rolls

I ALWAYS prefer my own home-made pasta. Apart from the flavour, I can make the quantity and size I require—it's far better in a recipe such as this to have a sheet size to fit perfectly in the baking dish. However, for convenience, the packet variety works well.

Serves 4–6

> 500 g ricotta
> 1 medium-size head broccoli, cooked until tender, chopped
> 6 spring onions, chopped
> 1/4 cup grated fresh Parmesan or cheese of your choice
> salt and freshly ground black pepper to taste
> 1/4 cup chopped fresh parsley or basil
> grated nutmeg
> 1 clove garlic, crushed
> 250 g home-made fresh lasagna sheets or 1 packet
>   pre-cooked lasagna sheets
> 100 g fresh mozzarella cheese, cubed
> a few black olives, pitted and chopped (optional)
> tomato sauce, see basics page 156

Place the ricotta in a large mixing bowl and add the broccoli and remaining ingredients, except the pasta, mozzarella and olives. Mash together and check for seasoning.

Cut the pasta sheets into squares and spread with the ricotta mixture. Roll up and place in an oiled baking dish.

Spoon the tomato sauce over the rolls and place cubed mozzarella down the centre of the sauce. Sprinkle with chopped olives and bake in a 250°C oven for about 20 minutes.

Serve hot.

Ricotta gnocchi with pumpkin sauce

GNOCCHI TAKES on a few forms, usually as an accompanying component of a meal. In this recipe, however, it is the leading light.

Serves 4 as an entrée

1 bunch spinach, very well washed
300 g ricotta
1 egg
$1/2$ cup freshly grated Parmesan cheese
3 tablespoons flour
pinch of freshly grated nutmeg
salt and freshly ground black pepper to taste
extra flour for dusting
melted butter
shaved Parmesan cheese
pumpkin sauce, see page 14

In a large saucepan, cook the spinach in a little boiling water until tender. Drain thoroughly, wrap in a cloth and squeeze until the spinach is very dry. Chop finely and place in a bowl. Add the ricotta, egg, Parmesan cheese, flour and nutmeg. Season to taste with salt and pepper and mix together well. Spoon out walnut-sized pieces of the mixture onto a floured board. Dust the balls lightly in extra flour.

Bring plenty of salted water to the boil in a shallow saucepan. Drop the gnocchi, a few at a time, into the water. As soon as they rise to the surface, remove them with a slotted spoon, draining well.

Arrange on a warm serving dish and keep warm. Pour over pumpkin sauce or melted butter and top with shaved Parmesan cheese

Chicken livers with gnocchi

CHICKEN livers are cheap yet jam-packed with flavour and nutrition. Make sure the green sacs (gall bladders) and extra sinew are removed.

Serves 4–6

> 3 cups milk
> 1 1/2 teaspoons salt
> pinch ground nutmeg
> 2/3 cup semolina
> 1 egg, lightly beaten
> 1 1/2 cups grated Parmesan cheese
> 60 g butter
> 2 tablespoons olive oil
> 250 g chicken livers, cleaned
> 1 onion, sliced
> a few sprigs thyme or sage
> a little brandy to flame (optional) ☞
> salt and freshly ground black pepper to taste
> rocket or some fresh young spinach leaves
> 2 tomatoes, finely diced
> dash sherry or balsamic vinegar

Bring the milk, salt and nutmeg to the boil. Reduce heat slightly and sprinkle in the semolina, stirring constantly. Combine the egg and 1 cup of the Parmesan cheese and add to the semolina mixture. Mix well.

Spread over a well-greased oven tray and refrigerate for 1 hour or until firm. Cut out into shapes (squares, diamonds, circles) and overlap in a greased baking dish. Top with butter and the remaining cheese and bake in a 180°C oven for 15–20 minutes.

Meanwhile, heat the oil in a non-stick frying-pan and add the livers and onion. Add the herbs and toss over a high heat until the onions and livers are browned. Flame with brandy, if desired, and season to taste with salt and pepper.

Arrange the rocket or spinach leaves on top of the gnocchi and place the livers in a line down the centre. Sprinkle with finely diced tomato and a little sherry and serve.

☞ *Hint: See Flaming Spirits, page 8*

Seafood

Steamed black bean fish with snow peas

FRESH, CLEAN flavours—the best way to enjoy seafood.

Serves 2

- 1 tablespoon Chinese fermented black beans (or black bean sauce)
- 1 tablespoon sherry, Shaohsing (Chinese cooking wine) or green ginger wine
- 2 pieces blue grenadier or similar fish
- 2 teaspoons peanut oil
- 1 cup snow peas or sugar snaps or a mixture of the two
- 1 teaspoon sugar
- 1 clove garlic, minced
- 2 tablespoons water
- 1/2 cup bean shoots
- 2 tablespoons water chestnuts, sliced or cut into fine strips
- 1/3 cup sherry, Shaohsing or green ginger wine, extra
- 1 teaspoon cornflour
- 2 teaspoons light soy sauce
- 2 teaspoons toasted sesame seeds ☞

Place the black beans in a bowl with the 1 tablespoon sherry and mash with a fork to make a paste. Place the fish on a plate or a piece of baking paper and smear with the black bean paste.

Steam or grill for about 5 minutes or until inside of the fish is white.

While the fish is steaming, heat the oil in a wok or frying-pan until very hot. Add the snow peas and stir-fry for 1 minute. Add the sugar and garlic and continue cooking for a further minute, then add the water, bean shoots and water chestnuts. Cover with a lid to allow the vegetables to finish cooking, about 1 more minute.

Mix the extra sherry with the cornflour and soy sauce and pour over vegetables. Toss until the sauce thickens and forms a glaze over the vegetables.

Spoon the vegetables onto heated serving plates and top with the fish. Sprinkle with toasted sesame seeds and serve.

☞ *Hint: See To Toast Sesame Seeds, page 15*

Thin-sliced tuna with roasted tomatoes

TUNA IS seasonal and can be expensive. This recipe also works with robustly flavoured fish such as sardines, mackerel or bonito.

Serves 4

> 8 Roma tomatoes, halved (sprinkle with a little sugar if
>   not ripe) ☞
> 1/2 cup olive oil
> salt and freshly ground black pepper to taste
> 8 slices stale bread
> 1/2 cup tightly packed fresh basil leaves
> 1 clove garlic, chopped
> 4 tuna steaks, about 2 cm thick
> 2 tablespoons lemon juice
> 1/2 small red onion, finely chopped
> extra fresh basil leaves for garnish
> a few small capers or olives

Place the tomatoes cut-side up on a baking tray. Drizzle with some of the olive oil, sprinkle with salt and pepper and bake in a 160°C oven for 1–1 1/2 hours, depending on the size of the tomatoes. They should shrivel a little but remain juicy.

Place the bread in a food processor with the basil, garlic and a pinch of salt and pepper. Process until crumbs form.

Put half the olive oil on a saucer and dip each tuna steak in the olive oil and then immediately in the breadcrumb mixture. Press the crumbs firmly onto the fish, shake off the excess and place the fish on a baking tray.

Cook under a very hot griller until golden brown. The fish is cooked as soon as the crumbs are brown. Turn once to cook the other side.

Slip the tomato flesh out of the skins into a bowl. Add the remaining olive oil, salt and pepper and lemon juice. Mash together.

Place the tuna on a serving plate and spoon over tomato mixture. Sprinkle with the finely chopped onion, extra basil leaves and capers or olives and serve.

☞ *Hint: See Roasting Tomatoes, page 16*

White fish steaks with fried capers and capsicum salad

CAPERS ARE the unopened flower pods from the caper bush. They are usually pickled in brine, however, they can come salted or even in oil. The smaller ones are the best. It is now commonplace to find a multitude of coloured capsicums. Buy as many different ones as you can for this recipe—the presentation will be spectacular. The capsicum salad keeps well in the fridge for up to a week—the herb and garlic character will become stronger.

Serves 4

> 4 kingfish or tuna steaks, 2–2.5 cm thick
> 1/2 cup olive oil
> salt and freshly ground black pepper to taste
> 2 tablespoons capers, squeezed dry of liquid in kitchen paper
> 4 sprigs rosemary or thyme
> 1/2 red capsicum, very finely sliced ☞
> 1/2 green capsicum, very finely sliced
> 1/2 yellow capsicum, very finely sliced
> 1/2 orange capsicum, very finely sliced
> 1/2 clove garlic, bruised
> pared rind and juice of 1/2 lemon

Trim the fish steaks if necessary. Brush with a little of the olive oil and sprinkle with salt and pepper. Allow to stand for around about 15 minutes.

Shallow-fry the capers in most of the remaining olive oil in a non-stick pan until they open and crisp, then remove.

Add the rosemary, sliced capsicum, garlic and lemon rind to the pan and take off the heat. Allow to infuse for 2 minutes, then add the lemon juice. Set aside.

Drain the pan if necessary. Reheat the pan until very hot and add the fish. Cook for 2 minutes on each side at the most, turning once only.

Place the fish on the centre of a warmed serving plate. Surround with the softened capsicum (having removed the herb, garlic and lemon rind). Sprinkle with fried capers and pepper and serve with a green salad of your choice.

☞ *Hint: See Buying Capsicums, page 5*

Stir-fried fish with Asian greens

ASIAN GREENS are a pretty good source of calcium and, with fish, generally regarded as our most digestible, healthy, low-fat source of protein. This makes for a tasty and nutritious meal. Serve with steamed rice or noodles.

Serves 6

750 g firm-fleshed fish fillets (gurnard, trevally or flake)
1 tablespoon sherry, Shaohsing (Chinese cooking wine),
   or green ginger wine
1 tablespoon cornflour
2 tablespoons soy sauce
1/4 cup peanut oil
2 cloves garlic, chopped
2 cm piece root ginger, grated or cut into very fine shreds ☞
1 red chilli, seeded and finely sliced (or two teaspoons chilli
   sauce)
1 cup spring onions, cut into 5 cm lengths
Asian greens such as choi sum, washed and cut into pieces
1 cup bean shoots
1/2 cup water
2 tablespoons oyster sauce
coriander leaves for serving

Trim the fish and remove bones with tweezers. Rinse and dry, then cut into bite-size pieces.

Mix the sherry, cornflour and soy sauce in a bowl, then add the fish and stir. Cover and leave to stand while preparing the vegetables.

Pour some oil into the wok and heat until very hot. Add the fish in small batches and gently toss for a minute or two, then remove to a plate.

When all the fish has been cooked, add some more oil to the wok if necessary and quickly stir-fry the garlic, ginger, chilli and spring onion before adding the choi sum and bean shoots. Toss for a minute, then add the water and cover. Allow to steam for one more minute, then remove the lid and add the oyster sauce. Thicken with cornflour if necessary, then return fish and gently toss to combine.

Sprinkle with coriander leaves and serve immediately.

☞ *Hint: See To Store Ginger, page 9*

Fish on the barbecue

ACCOMPANY this quick fish dish with char-grilled vegetables.

Serves 4

> 4 medium-size fish cutlets about 2 cm thick (trevally or blue-
> eye cod)
> 2 tablespoons peanut oil
> 2 cm piece root ginger, peeled and grated
> 1-2 red chillies, seeded and finely chopped ☞
> handful of fresh coriander, stems finely chopped and leaves
> set aside
> 2 tablespoons soy sauce
> 2 tablespoons sherry, Shaohsing (Chinese cooking wine), or
> green ginger wine

Dry fish with a paper towel.

Combine oil, ginger, chilli, chopped coriander stems, soy sauce and sherry. Brush fish lightly with this baste.

Heat the barbecue hot plate or char-grill until hot. Brush with some peanut oil.

Place fish on the grill and cook for 3–4 minutes on each side, turning once only. Brush with the baste, scatter with coriander leaves and serve.

☞ *Hint: See Preparing Chillies, page 5*

Fish chowder

A HEARTY dish, ideal for cold winter nights. Use cod or flake as they don't break up when cooked.

Serves 6–8

  1 bunch spinach, trimmed and well washed (optional)
  3 tablespoons butter
  1 leek, cut into rings and well washed
  1 stick celery, chopped
  1 litre water
  2 Pontiac potatoes, scrubbed and cubed
  1 bay leaf
  salt and freshly ground white pepper to taste
  500 g firm white fish fillet
  12 mussels, scrubbed and beards removed ☞
  1 cob corn or 1 cup frozen corn kernels
  1/2 cup cream
  1/2 cup chopped fresh parsley for garnish

Blanch the spinach by cooking lightly in a steamer or in the microwave. Run under cold water, then squeeze out the excess moisture. Divide between serving bowls.

Heat the butter in a large saucepan and soften the leek and celery over a medium heat.

Add the water, potatoes, bay leaf, salt and pepper and bring to the boil. Simmer for about 8 minutes. Add fish, mussels and corn and simmer gently for a further 5 minutes. Discard any mussels which have not opened. Season to taste, add cream, remove bay leaf and ladle onto the spinach in the serving bowls. Sprinkle with parsley and serve with crusty bread.

☞ Hint: See To Clean Mussels, page 11

Mussels with dry spices

MUSSELS SHOULD be small to medium in size, shiny black and closed when bought. The aroma, when fresh, is rich, sweet and very appealing. If you notice any hint of unpleasant odour—don't buy them. As they are cooked together one or two spoiled mussels will affect the whole batch and the all-important juices.

Serves 4

> 1 kg mussels, cleaned and beards removed ☞
> 1 cup water
> 2 tablespoons coriander seeds
> 2 teaspoons cumin seeds
> 2 tablespoons sesame seeds
> 1 teaspoon paprika
> 1/2 teaspoon freshly ground black pepper
> 1/4 cup unblanched almonds, roasted
> 1/2 teaspoon castor sugar
> 2 cups thinly sliced vegetables (leeks, carrots and zucchini)
> salt to taste
> Tabasco sauce
> juice of 1 lime
> fresh coriander leaves

Put the cleaned mussels into a large saucepan with water. Cover the pan and place over high heat and steam the mussels, shaking the pan every now and again, for 5–6 minutes until they have opened. Drain and reserve liquor. Discard any unopened shells.

Place the coriander, cumin and sesame seeds in a small pan and dry-roast over a low heat until the mixture is fragrant. Add the paprika and pepper and roast for another minute.

Use a mortar and pestle or a coffee mill to grind the spices and almonds to a coarse powder. Add the sugar. Set aside.

Place the thinly sliced vegetables and 1 cup of the mussel liquor in a stainless steel or non-stick frying-pan with a lid. With the lid on, steam over a high heat until the vegetables are barely softened, about 3 minutes.

Add the mussels and adjust the liquid by adding more liquor if the vegies look dry. Return the lid and steam for a further minute to warm the mussels. Do not overcook or they will shrink. Add salt, Tabasco and lime juice to taste.

Serve the mussels and vegetables in mounds on plates or in deep bowls, sprinkled with coriander leaves and dry-spice mix.

☞ *Hint: See To Clean Mussels, page 11*

Tuna jack-in-a-box

THIS IS a great way to make a simple meal into something special in order to fool the kids!

Serves 4

1 stale, unsliced, square loaf
melted butter or olive oil for brushing
1 leek or 4 spring onions, well washed and chopped
1 cup whole button mushrooms, cleaned
1 cob corn, kernels removed
60 g butter, extra
$1/4$ cup flour
1 $1/2$ cups cold milk
salt and freshly ground pepper to taste
425 g can tuna in spring water, drained
1 tablespoon chopped fresh dill (optional)
$1/2$ bunch spinach, cooked and drained
dash of dry sherry (optional)
squeeze of lemon juice (optional)
extra chopped fresh dill for garnish (optional)
a little chopped red capsicum for garnish (optional)

Cut the bread evenly into four portions and remove the crusts. Cut a slice from the top of each block to form a lid.

With a narrow-bladed sharp knife, cut a square in the block about 1 cm from each edge.

Insert the knife on one side about 1 cm from the base and make a cut parallel to the bottom—this should release the inside leaving a hollow case. Reserve the discarded centre for breadcrumbs.

Brush the case and lid with the melted butter and bake in a 150°C oven for about 15 minutes or until crisp and golden brown.

Cook the leek, mushrooms and corn kernels in half the extra butter for a few minutes until they are just cooked but not brown.

In a separate saucepan, melt the remaining butter over a medium heat. When the foaming subsides, add the flour and stir well for about 2 minutes—do not brown. Add the cold milk a little at a time, stirring constantly until smooth and thickened. Simmer the sauce for 5 minutes, then season to taste with salt and pepper.

Fold through the tuna, dill, spinach and the sautéed vegetables, a little sherry and lemon juice if using and heat through. Spoon generously into the bread cases. Sprinkle with extra dill and a little chopped red capsicum and top with a lid.

☞ *Hint: See To Make Breadcrumbs, page 4*

Hot smoked ocean trout

DO THIS outdoors—it can completely fill the kitchen with smoke. Untreated wood chips are readily available from barbecue stores.

Serves 4

> ¹/₄ cup untreated wood chips, such as fruit wood, oregon or hickory
> 4 ocean trout or salmon cutlets

For the topping

¹/₂ cup snow peas, blanched
¹/₂ cup bean shoots, blanched
2 tablespoons Thai-style sweet chilli sauce
1 teaspoon sesame oil
2 teaspoons lemon or lime juice
sesame seeds, toasted (or black sesame seeds) ☞

Place a double layer of foil in the bottom of a wok and sprinkle with the wood chips. Place an oiled rack over the wood and lay the fish cutlets over it. Cover with a lid and cook over a high heat for about 6 minutes—it is fine for the fish to be slightly underdone. Do not remove the lid more than is necessary or the smoke will go everywhere.

To prepare the topping: Cut the snow peas into fine strips and mix with the bean shoots. Combine the remaining ingredients, except sesame seeds, to make a dressing and toss this with the snow peas and bean shoots. Arrange some of this mixture over each ocean trout cutlet. Sprinkle with sesame seeds and serve.

☞ *Hint: See To Toast Sesame Seeds, page 15*

Poultry

Moroccan chicken couscous

MOROCCAN dishes have a wonderfully exotic fragrance. If you can get hold of them, preserved lemons, chopped and stirred through, really lift this dish.

Serves 6–8

500 g couscous
a knob of butter
1/4 cup olive oil
1 kg chicken thighs and drumsticks
2 medium-size onions, chopped
2 cloves garlic, chopped
1 teaspoon ground cumin
1 teaspoon ground coriander
1 teaspoon ground ginger
1 teaspoon sweet paprika
pinch of saffron (optional)
1 cinnamon stick
6 cups water
300 g can peeled tomatoes
2 carrots, peeled and cut into chunks
1 turnip, peeled and cut into chunks
375 g can chickpeas (or 1 cup fresh, soaked overnight and
    boiled until tender)
2 zucchini, peeled and cut into chunks
salt and freshly ground black pepper to taste
fresh parsley or coriander leaves for garnish

Harissa

50 g dried red chillies ☞
3 cloves garlic, peeled
1 teaspoon salt
1 1/4 tablespoons ground coriander
1 teaspoon dried mint leaves or 1 tablespoon fresh mint leaves
1 1/2 tablespoons ground cumin
1/3 cup olive oil

Make up the couscous according to the directions on the packet. Stir through butter and leave to stand.

Heat the olive oil in a large, heavy-based saucepan and add the chicken pieces. Cook, turning occasionally until brown, then remove and set aside.

Add the onion, garlic and spices to the pan and sweat until softened and fragrant. Add the water, tomatoes, carrots and turnips, then return the chicken to the pan. Season to taste with salt and pepper. Simmer for 20 minutes, adding the chickpeas and zucchini pieces half way through the cooking time.

Heap the couscous onto a large platter and arrange the chicken and vegetables on top. Ladle over some of the broth and serve the rest separately. Sprinkle with parsley or coriander leaves and serve with harissa.

To prepare the harissa: Wearing rubber gloves, split the chillies and remove the seeds. Soften in hot water for 1 hour. Drain.

Process the garlic, salt, coriander, mint and cumin with the chillies to form a paste. Drizzle in the olive oil and store in a jar.

☞ *Hint: See Preparing Chillies, page 5*

Chicken biryani

THIS DISH is terrific for an informal dinner party. Serve it with a selection of sambals and crisp pappadums.

Serves 6–8

- 1/4 cup oil or ghee
- 1 kg chicken pieces, skin removed
- 1 onion, chopped
- 1 3/4 cups jasmine fragrant long-grain rice, soaked in water for one hour, then well-drained
- 3 tablespoons biryani paste
- 1 teaspoon salt
- 2 cloves garlic, minced
- 2 cups water
- 1/4 teaspoon saffron strands
- 2 tablespoons milk
- raisins
- blanched roasted almonds
- 4 hard-boiled eggs, sliced
- 1 cup of caramelised onion ☞

Heat half the oil in a large saucepan and brown the chicken pieces. Remove and set aside.

Add the onion and rice to the pan and cook until the onion is pale gold. Add the biryani paste, salt and garlic and fry for 1 minute, then return the chicken pieces to the pan. Pour over the water and bring to the boil. Reduce the heat, cover and simmer gently for 20 minutes. Heat the saffron in the milk and pour over the rice and stir.

Fry the raisins and almonds in the remaining oil. Pile the rice and chicken onto a heated serving platter. Arrange the egg slices over the rice and top with the raisins, almonds and onions.

☞ Hint: See To Caramelise Onions, page 12

Creamy cajun-spiced chicken

THE PRESENTATION of this dish is slightly old-fashioned.
Nonetheless, it's colorful and the flavours work well.

Serves 4

- 2 large onions, cut into rings
- 3 sticks celery, julienned
- 2 capsicums, sliced into 3 cm thick strips
- 4 chicken breast fillets, skin removed
- 4 slices smoked ham
- 4 skewers
- 1 tablespoon cajun spices or combine 1/2 teaspoon onion
  powder, 1/2 teaspoon garlic powder, 1/2 teaspoon
  cayenne, 1/2 teaspoon ground cumin, 1/2 teaspoon finely
  ground black pepper, 1/2 teaspoon ground oregano
- 2 tablespoons oil
- 250 ml cream
- 2 tablespoons lemon juice

Blanch the onions, celery and capsicums and refresh in cold water.

Slice each fillet open to form a pocket. Divide the vegetables and ham
evenly between the fillets in layers. Close the fillets and secure with
skewers.

Gently toss the fillets in the cajun spices and coat thoroughly.

Heat the oil in a large frying-pan and cook fillets until golden brown
on the outside. Add the cream and lemon juice to the pan and stir to
combine flavours and coat the chicken.

Simmer for several minutes more until chicken is cooked and sauce is
slightly thickened, then serve.

☞ Hint: See To Blanch Vegetables, page 3

Beggar's chicken

THIS IS a dramatic dish, bound to impress. It is not challenging from a skills point of view—the only drawback is the time involved, but it's worth it.

Serves 4

   3 cups plain flour
   2 cups cooking salt
   1 1/4 cups water (approx.)
   1 no. 16 chicken
   a little oil
   1/4 cup dark soy sauce
   4 spring onions, roughly chopped
   2 cloves garlic, crushed
   3 cm piece root ginger, roughly chopped ☞
   2 small red chillies, roughly chopped
   1/4 teaspoon five spice powder (optional)
   1 teaspoon sugar
   2 tablespoons sherry, Shaohsing (Chinese rice wine), or green
      ginger wine
   cotton string

Preheat the oven to 230°C.

Place flour and salt in a large mixing bowl and mix well. Gradually mix in the water to form a firm dough, adding a little extra water if required. Set aside.

Wash and thoroughly dry the chicken and remove the fat from inside the cavity. Pull the neck skin tightly underneath and tuck the wing tips under so they hold the skin in place.

Oil two large sheets of foil and place them in a cross formation over a plate or bowl. Place the chicken in the centre of the foil and brush with some of the soy sauce.

Place the spring onions, garlic, ginger, chilli, remaining soy sauce, five spice powder, sugar and sherry in a small bowl and combine. Carefully pour the mixture inside the cavity of the chicken and tie the legs tightly together with cotton string. Wrap the chicken tightly and securely in the foil.

Roll out the salt dough to a thickness of 1 cm and large enough to encase the chicken. Place the chicken in the centre and fold over the dough, sealing the edges well with water.

Wet your hands and smooth over the outside of the dough making sure there are no cracks or holes for steam to escape.

Place on a baking tray in the oven for 1 hour. Reduce the heat to 200°C and cook for a further 2 hours.

To serve, break open the salt crust with a hammer or mallet and discard. Carefully peel back the foil and serve the chicken with the juices and some rice.

☞ *Hint: See To Store Ginger, page 9*

Chinese restaurant-style lemon chicken

WE ALL have those occasions when our dinner guests are less experienced diners and to be the perfect host, we want to prepare something familiar and not too challenging. Well, here it is...

Serves 4

4 chicken breast fillets, skin removed
1/3 cup self-raising flour
1/3 cup cornflour
1/3 cup ice-cold water
pinch of salt
1 egg
juice of 1/2 lemon
1 teaspoon sesame oil
peanut oil for deep-frying
lemon slices for garnish

Lemon sauce

1/2 cup chicken stock
1 tablespoon mild honey (or to taste)
1 teaspoon grated fresh ginger
1/4 cup lemon juice
2 teaspoons cornflour
1 tablespoon water
1/4 teaspoon chilli paste
4 spring onions, cut into 3 cm pieces
salt and freshly ground black pepper to taste

Flatten the chicken fillets slightly with a mallet.

Place the self-raising flour and cornflour in a mixing bowl and add the water, salt, egg, lemon juice and sesame oil. Whisk together until smooth. Coat the chicken in this batter and deep-fry in hot oil until golden and cooked through.

Drain well on absorbent paper. Place in a warm oven.

To make the lemon sauce: In a small saucepan bring stock, honey, ginger and lemon juice to the boil. Blend the cornflour with the water and use to thicken the sauce. When the sauce is simmering, stir in the chilli paste and the spring onions. Season to taste with salt and pepper.

Cut each chicken breast into three or four strips and arrange on a serving dish with sliced lemon. Pour over hot lemon sauce and serve with steamed rice.

☞ *Hint: See Deep-frying, page 7*

Chicken lasagne

A VARIATION on the theme, which keeps and reheats well.

Serves 6–8

- 1 tablespoon olive oil
- 750 g minced chicken ☞
- 1 onion, finely chopped
- 1 clove garlic, minced
- 425 g can peeled tomatoes, crushed
- 140 g tub tomato paste
- salt and freshly ground black pepper to taste
- 1 bay leaf
- 1 kg ricotta
- a little freshly grated nutmeg
- 1/2 cup chopped fresh parsley
- 1 packet fresh lasagne noodles
- 150 g shaved or thinly sliced ham
- 1 cup grated mozzarella cheese

Heat the oil in a non-stick saucepan and quickly brown the chicken mince. Remove from the pan. Add the onion and garlic to the pan and sweat until the onion softens. Return the chicken to the pan and add the tomatoes and tomato paste. Season with salt and pepper, add the bay leaf and simmer for about 15 minutes. Place the ricotta in a mixing bowl and season with salt, pepper and nutmeg. Add the chopped parsley and mash together.

Spread a little chicken mixture in the base of a lasagne dish and top with a layer of pasta. Spread half of the remaining chicken sauce over the pasta. Top with another layer of pasta, then spread with half the ricotta mixture and half the ham. Top with more pasta and repeat with remaining chicken mixture and ricotta mixture.

Top with the remaining ham and mozzarella. Bake in a 180°C oven for about 40 minutes, then serve with salad.

☞ *Hint: See To Mince Chicken, page 5*

Chicken with grapes

HERE'S A quick meal with a classic combination of flavours—you can't go wrong.

Serves 2

- 1 teaspoon olive oil
- 2 chicken breast fillets, skin removed
- 1/2 cup grapes (split and seeded if they have seeds, and skinned if desired) ☞
- 1/4 cup dry vermouth
- salt and freshly ground black pepper to taste
- 30 g cold butter, chopped
- a few tarragon leaves

Heat the oil in a frying-pan and quickly brown the chicken fillets on both sides. Reduce the heat and continue cooking until the chicken is done. Remove from the pan and keep warm.

Sauté the grapes in the oil in the pan. Splash in the vermouth and shake the pan to dissolve the caramelised juices. Season with salt and pepper and swirl in the butter a little at a time. Pour over the chicken, sprinkle with tarragon leaves and serve.

☞ *Hint: See To Peel Grapes, page 9*

Chicken and okra gumbo

GUMBOS ARE thick, flavour-filled, rib-sticking and satisfying broths. Actually, one of the best one-pot dishes you can prepare for a cold winter night. The great and forgiving aspect of this recipe is that most vegetables and meats qualify to be included in this classic southern American dish. Experiment for yourself...it's hard to go wrong.

Serves 4–8

1 medium-size chicken
1 teaspoon salt
1/2 teaspoon chilli powder or cayenne
plain flour
salt and freshly ground black pepper to taste
2/3 cup oil
2 onions, chopped
2 sticks celery, chopped
4 cloves garlic, chopped
1 cup chicken or turkey sausage, cut into small pieces
2 large red capsicums, roasted, peeled, seeded and diced
1 teaspoon chopped fresh thyme
1/2–1 teaspoon chilli powder, extra
1 cup okra, chopped ☞
2 tomatoes, peeled and chopped
6 3/4–7 1/2 cups chicken stock
1 1/2 cups hot, cooked rice
2 tablespoons chopped spring onions for garnish
2 tablespoons chopped fresh parsley for garnish

Take all the chicken meat from the bones and cut it into small cubes, about 1 cm square. Put the chicken in a bowl with the salt and chilli powder and leave in a cool place while you prepare the other ingredients.

Season the flour with salt and pepper and roll the chicken pieces in it. Heat the oil in a heavy-based pan, and fry the chicken pieces in three batches; they should be just slightly browned. Take them out with a slotted spoon and drain on a paper towel. Remove some of the oil from the pan leaving about 3 tablespoons and the flour sediment at the bottom. In this, fry the onions, celery, garlic, sausage and diced capsicum, stirring constantly, for 3 minutes. Add the thyme and extra chilli powder while continuing to stir for 1 minute more.

Add the okra, chopped tomatoes and chicken meat. Stir again, cover the pan, and simmer for 5 minutes. Add half the stock and continue to simmer, covered, for 50–60 minutes. Add the rest of the stock, adjust the seasoning and continue to cook until the gumbo has the consistency you want; this can be as soupy or as thick as you choose.

Divide the rice among serving bowls, and serve the gumbo ladled over the top, garnished with chopped spring onions and parsley.

☞ *Hint: See Okra, page 12*

Peking duck pancakes

A SPECIAL dish for a special occasion. Ask your local Chinese restaurant, or Chinese barbecue shop, to prepare the Peking duck for you. You may have to order it some time in advance, so check early.

1 bunch spring onions
1 Peking duck, purchased from a Chinese restaurant
1 jar hoi sin sauce (preferably from Hong Kong)

Pancake batter

650 ml milk
250 g flour
pinch salt
4 eggs
20 ml double cream
30 g butter

To prepare pancakes: Boil the milk and set aside to cool. In a bowl, combine the flour and salt. Add the eggs, two at a time, mixing in well. Add one third of the milk and beat well. Pour in the cream and the rest of the milk, beating until the batter is smooth. Stand for 30 minutes before cooking.

Trim the roots from the spring onions and cut 10 cm lengths from the bottom of the bunch and reserve. Finely chop some of the remaining green part to make about 1/2 cup and stir through batter.

Rub your crepe pan or frying-pan with the butter, add some batter and tilt the pan so that the batter coats the bottom. Cook for 1–2 minutes each side, tossing or using a palate knife to turn. Remove from pan and keep warm while making the rest of the pancakes.

Shred the green end of the reserved spring onion sticks with a pin and place in a bowl of cold water for about 20 minutes to curl the ends.

Cut slices of meat from the duck, including the skin.

Lay out the pancakes and spread with a little hoi sin sauce. Top with a few pieces of duck meat and fold into quarters.

Arrange on a platter, cover with foil and warm through in the oven just before serving. Slip a spring onion brush into each pancake and serve.

☞ *Hint: See Pancakes and Crepes, page 12*

Asian-style chicken legs with fried noodles

THE FLAVOURS in this dish have a delightful complexity, yet it's extremely simple to create.

Serves 4

1 kg chicken legs, preferably corn-fed
1 cup water
5 cm piece root ginger, sliced
1 clove garlic, chopped
roots and stems from 1 bunch coriander
1 small piece star anise
1 strip lemon rind
1 small onion, finely chopped
1 teaspoon peanut oil
handful of deep-fried Asian noodles ☞
1 clove garlic, extra, finely chopped
1 teaspoon finely chopped ginger, extra
1 small red chilli, seeded and finely chopped
1 tablespoon hoi sin sauce
1 tablespoon chopped fresh coriander leaves
1 teaspoon lemon juice

Place the chicken legs in a small saucepan with the water, ginger, garlic, coriander, star anise and lemon rind. Cover, slowly bring to a simmer and poach gently for about 30 minutes.

Meanwhile, cook the onion in the oil until it is lightly browned. Place the noodles in a serving bowl and top with the chicken legs. Strain the poaching stock over the onions and add the extra garlic and ginger, chilli, hoi sin sauce, coriander leaves and lemon juice. Quickly swirl together, pour over the chicken and serve straight away.

☞ Hint: See To Deep-fry Asian Noodles, page 7

Meat

Thai pork curry with eggplant

THE DIFFERENCE between home-made and shop-bought curry pastes is immeasurable. These days most Asian ingredients are readily available from specialty markets in our major cities. Since the quality of the fresh Asian produce is so high, it's a worthwhile exercise making your own Asian pastes and condiments.

Don't be put off by the hand grinding with the mortar and pestle. You will still get an excellent result by using a powerful coffee grinder for the dry ingredients and a blender for the paste itself. Just remember that the mortar and pestle do a better job in releasing the oils trapped within these ingredients, vastly improving the flavour and fragrance.

This is a delicious, authentic recipe, and very easy to make once you have sourced all the exotic spices.

If you appreciate the bitterness, use the little green pea eggplant, but don't chop them.

Serves 6

Curry paste

2 teaspoons dried chilli flakes
1 small red onion, chopped
3 cloves garlic, crushed
2 tablespoons chopped fresh lemon grass ☞
1 dried Kaffir lime leaf
1 teaspoon grated lime zest
1 teaspoon paprika
$1/2$ teaspoon turmeric
$1/2$ teaspoon cumin seeds
2 teaspoons oil
$1/2$ teaspoon shrimp paste, toasted
1 teaspoon laos powder
2 teaspoons chopped fresh coriander root
lime juice to taste

Curry

¹/₄ cup coconut cream

750 g pork fillet, finely sliced

2 cups coconut milk

1 medium-size eggplant, chopped into cubes

1 tablespoon fish sauce

1 ¹/₂ teaspoons grated fresh ginger

2 teaspoons palm sugar

3 small green chillies, sliced

3 small red chillies, sliced

¹/₄ cup fresh Thai basil leaves, shredded

To prepare the curry paste: Grind all the ingredients together using a mortar and pestle until fairly smooth. You can keep this paste in the fridge for a week or two in a screw-top glass jar.

To prepare the curry: Combine the curry paste and coconut cream in a heavy-based saucepan and cook until fragrant, about 1 minute. Add the pork slices and simmer for 5 minutes.

Add the coconut milk, eggplant, fish sauce, ginger, sugar and chillies. Bring to the boil and then simmer, uncovered, for 1 hour or until the pork is tender. Just before serving stir in the basil and adjust seasoning and sharpness with extra lime juice.

☞ *Hint: See Buying and Preparing Lemon Grass, page 10*

Rolled pork with spinach and chestnut stuffing

CHESTNUTS are a hoot...the ritual of toasting and roasting them is a bit of fun and then of course the smooth, rich texture is one of those autumn–winter treats not to be missed. Don't buy the very first chestnuts to hit the market—they're always double the price of the supplies which come in a few weeks later.

Serves 4

> 4 pork schnitzels
> 100 g fresh chestnuts
> 1/2 teaspoon coriander seeds
> 1 teaspoon mustard seeds
> oil for frying
> 100 g fresh button mushrooms, sliced
> 200 g fresh spinach leaves, washed and dried
> salt and freshly ground black pepper to taste
> 2 tablespoons Madeira
> 1/3 cup reduced-fat cream
> 1 tablespoon wholegrain mustard
> toothpicks or butcher's twine ☞

Preheat the oven to 190°C.

If the schnitzels are very thick, flatten them out by covering them with plastic wrap and beating them firmly with a mallet or rolling pin.

Using a sharp knife, cut a slit in the hard outer shell of the chestnuts and roast them in the oven for 20–30 minutes. Cool and shell, removing the second skin. Chop roughly.

In a hot frying-pan, lightly dry-roast the coriander and mustard seeds. Crush the seeds using a mortar and pestle.

Heat some oil in the pan. Add the mushrooms and sauté until they begin to soften. Add the spinach leaves and heat through until they wilt. Remove from heat.

Combine the mushroom and spinach with the seeds and seasonings. Divide the mixture evenly between the schnitzels and spread over one surface. Roll the meat up and secure with a toothpick or butcher's twine.

Heat some more oil in a non-stick frying-pan and brown each schnitzel on all sides, including both ends. Place schnitzels in baking dish and bake for 10–15 minutes. Remove once cooked through and cover with foil. Allow to rest for 5 minutes.

Quickly add the Madeira, cream and mustard to the pan juices and stir well over medium heat to make a sauce. Remove the toothpicks or string from the pork and serve with the sauce.

☞ *Hint: See Tying Meats, page 11*

Barbecued pork with peach salsa and zucchini couscous

THE PEACH salsa in this recipe balances the richness of the pork and provides colour contrast on the plate. Don't make the salsa too far in advance.

Serves 4

- 1 tablespoon peppercorns
- 1 teaspoon cumin seeds
- 1 teaspoon coriander seeds
- 4 pork butterfly medallions
- 2 tablespoons olive oil
- 1 clove garlic, crushed

Peach salsa

- 2 ripe freestone peaches (or mango), finely cubed
- 3 tablespoons chopped fresh coriander leaves (optional)
- 3 tablespoons chopped fresh mint leaves
- 1 fresh green chilli or 1 teaspoon chilli sauce or paste
- salt and freshly ground black pepper to taste
- juice of 1 lemon or lime
- 1 tablespoon peanut or light olive oil
- 1/2 red onion, finely chopped

Place the peppercorns, cumin and coriander seeds on a wooden board and crush with the bottom of a clean saucepan or use a mortar and pestle. Place the pork medallions in a dish with the olive oil, cracked spices and garlic and leave to stand for an hour or so.

To prepare the peach salsa: Mix all the salsa ingredients together in a bowl and allow to stand in the fridge for about an hour.

Barbecue the pork for about 4 minutes on each side or until the meat is done to your liking.

Serve pork accompanied by the peach salsa and couscous mixed with sautéed zucchini and garlic.

☞ Hint: See Meats, page 11

Beef and bean red curry

CORIANDER, red curry paste and coconut milk combine to give this curry a classic Thai flavour. The characteristic feature is the fragrance, which can only be achieved with the freshest ingredients and high quality curry paste.

2 teaspoons coriander seeds
1 tablespoon vegetable oil
1 onion, chopped
2 tablespoons red curry paste
1 clove garlic, crushed
400 ml coconut milk
750 g braising beef (round or flank), cubed
200 g fresh green beans
dash lime or lemon juice
fish sauce to taste
salt and freshly ground black pepper to taste

In a small frying-pan, dry-roast the coriander seeds, then crush or grind them. Heat the oil in a large saucepan pan and sauté the onion until lightly browned. Add curry paste and garlic and cook, stirring continuously, for 5 minutes. Add the coconut milk, bring to the boil, then add the meat and coriander seeds.

Simmer, uncovered, for 1–1 1/2 hours or until the meat is tender.

Top and tail the beans and cut into 5 cm lengths. Add to the curry and cook until the beans are tender. Season with the lime juice, fish sauce and salt and pepper.

Serve with jasmine fragrant rice or an alternative aromatic long-grain rice such as Basmati cooked by the absorption method.

☞ *Hint: See Rice, Absorption Method, page 158*

Beef and sauerkraut hot pot

THIS IS a variation on an age-old recipe and needless to say it's a real rib-sticker, great for a winter party of 12 people. The added bonus is that it should be prepared well in advance.

This recipe uses sauerkraut, which is made by layering shredded fresh cabbage in a large earthenware crock with salt and spices and weighting it for about three weeks, during which time the cabbage ferments. However, I have found that a similar and easier result can be achieved if you mix equal quantities of canned sauerkraut and shredded fresh cabbage and leave it, covered with plastic wrap, in the fridge overnight.

Serves 12

- 1 large onion, diced
- 2 tablespoons olive oil
- 2 cloves garlic, chopped ☞
- 1 1/2 tablespoons paprika
- 2 tablespoons tomato paste
- 1 1/2 kg chuck steak, cubed
- 750 g tomatoes, peeled and chopped
- 1 green capsicum, diced
- 1 red capsicum, diced
- 1.5 kg sauerkraut (1/2 canned, 1/2 fresh cabbage)
- 2 hot continental sausages (csabai), cut into thin rings
- 3/4 cup sour cream

Fry onion in oil in a large saucepan. When the onion is soft add garlic and fry for 1 minute. Stir in the paprika, tomato paste, steak, tomatoes and capsicums. Stir well. Cover and simmer for 1 1/2 hours until the meat is tender.

Divide sauerkraut and sausage into three portions and the beef mixture into two. Take a large casserole dish and layer firstly sauerkraut and sausage, then beef mixture.

Repeat and finish with sauerkraut and sausage layer. Cover and bake for 1 ½ hours at 150°C. Refrigerate overnight.

Next day, bake for 1 ½ hours more at 150°C, removing the lid for the last half hour. Spread the sour cream on top and serve directly from the casserole.

☞ *Hint: See How To Prepare Garlic, page 8*

Balti-style lamb chops with fragrant rice

BALTI COOKING is very communal. Try to get hold of some naan bread (traditional Indian bread) and plonk piles of bread and curry in the centre of the table so everyone can tuck in.

The combination of the mild curry paste and yoghurt in this dish enhances the natural flavour of the lamb and leaves the meat succulent and tender.

Serves 6

   30 g ghee or oil
   8 lamb chops (e.g. chump or forequarter)
   1 onion, sliced
   1/3 cup mild curry paste
   2 bay leaves
   1 teaspoon crushed garlic
   1/3 cup plain yoghurt
   4 medium-size tomatoes, peeled and chopped ☞
   1 cup water

Fragrant rice

   1 1/4 cups Basmati rice
   1 tablespoon vegetable oil
   1 medium onion, chopped
   440 ml hot water
   a pinch of saffron strands
   1 tablespoon coriander leaves, torn

Heat the ghee in a wok or Balti pan. Add the chops and cook until well browned. Remove and set aside.

Add the onion and cook for a few minutes before adding the curry paste, bay leaves and garlic. Cook for a few minutes, then add the yoghurt and fry for 1 minute. Return the chops, add the tomatoes and water and leave to simmer for 25 minutes or until the meat is tender. Add more water if necessary and adjust the seasoning.

To prepare the fragrant rice: Rinse rice well. Heat oil and saute onion in a heavy-based saucepan until golden brown. Add washed, drained rice and saute, stirring, for 1 minute. Add water, stir and boil for 15 minutes. Add saffron, lower the heat, cover and continue to cook for a further 5 minutes.

Fork through coriander and serve with lamb accompanied by a salad made with tomatoes, onion, salt, pepper and sugar.

☞ *Hint: See Peeling Tomatoes, page 17*

Braised lamb shanks with mushrooms and Madeira

MADEIRA IS a sweet Portuguese fortified wine which gives a wonderful, full-bodied flavour to meat braises. The same recipe works beautifully if you use oxtail in place of the lamb shanks. Avoid using oyster or enoki mushrooms as they will collapse in this sauce.

Serves 4–8

8 lamb shanks (have your butcher saw off the knuckles)
50 ml olive oil
salt and freshly ground black pepper to taste
8 unpeeled cloves garlic
1 bay leaf
1 sprig thyme
250 ml Madeira or port
water or beef stock
1 tomato, seeds removed, flesh cut into small dice
chopped fresh chives or parsley for garnish

Sauce

1 small onion, finely diced
500 g shiitake, Swiss brown or common button mushrooms
1 tablespoon butter
1 tablespoon chopped fresh sage
1/2 cup Madeira or port

In a roasting pan large enough to hold the 8 shanks, brown them all in olive oil. Sprinkle with salt and pepper. Poke the garlic, bay leaf and thyme in and under the shanks, pour in the Madeira and then enough water (or better still beef stock if you have it) for the liquid to come half way up the shanks. Bring to the boil, cover tightly with foil and slow braise in a 140°C oven for 2 1/2 hours. Remove the shanks, then strain the liquid to reserve as a stock, skimming off excess fat.

To make the sauce: Fry the onion and mushrooms (sliced or whole depending on your preference) in half the butter over high heat, tossing frequently until they brown nicely. Mix through the sage, then pour in the Madeira and about 250 ml of the reserved lamb stock. Boil this down until it approaches a sauce consistency, then stir in the remaining butter.

Pour the sauce over the warmed lamb shanks and serve, allowing 1 or 2 per person. Finally, scatter over the diced tomato and a sprinkling of chives or parsley.

Note: You usually end up with too much lamb stock. The remainder can be frozen for later use. It has a fabulous, rich, meaty flavour and is perfect for making a quick sauce to enliven a simple dish of say, grilled lamb.

Crumbed lamb cutlets with garlic potato purée

DOUBLE LAMB cutlets work well—they take a little extra cooking but will be more moist in the centre. If you like the crumb coating, and also if you're using double cutlets, try double crumbing—quite simply repeat the crumbing process.

Serves 4

 4 slices sour dough or coarse bread
 1 clove garlic, peeled
 grated rind of 1 lemon
 a few sprigs of parsley
 2 teaspoons fresh rosemary leaves
 salt and freshly ground pepper to taste
 8 lamb cutlets, well-trimmed
 a little plain flour
 1 egg, beaten
 a little olive oil for frying
 4 potatoes, peeled and cubed
 4 cloves garlic, extra, peeled ☞
 40 g butter
 100 ml cream
 1/2 cup hot, cooked spinach

Break the bread into pieces and place in a food processor with the garlic, lemon rind, parsley, rosemary, salt and pepper. Process to crumbs and pour onto a plate.

Flatten each chop slightly with the palm of your hand. Coat the cutlets first in flour, then egg, then crumb mixture, shaking off any excess. Allow to chill in the fridge if possible.

Pan-fry the cutlets gently in olive oil until lightly browned.

Meanwhile, cut the potatoes into cubes, place into a saucepan, cover with cold water, season with salt and add the garlic. Simmer until the potatoes are tender. Drain and pass through a sieve or a mouli. Boil the butter and cream together and gently work into the potatoes. Season with salt and pepper.

Fold through the spinach and mound onto a plate. Top with lamb cutlets and serve.

☞ *Hint: See How To Prepare Garlic, page 8*

Eggplant stuffed fillets of lamb

LAMB AND eggplant are natural companions in many Mediterranean countries. The texture of lamb sits well with the smoothness of eggplant. When stuffing a small piece of meat like this, it is important to keep the stuffing moist with olive oil to prevent it drying out. The other general point to note with brief cooking of small quantities of meat is that the stuffing needs to be cooked beforehand as there is not enough cooking time in this recipe to do the job.

Serves 4

> 2 medium-size eggplant ☞
> 75 ml olive oil
> 1 small onion, very finely diced
> 1/2 teaspoon dried Greek oregano
> 1/2 red chilli, very finely chopped
> juice of 1/2 lemon
> 1/2 teaspoon each salt and pepper combined
> 1 cup soft fresh breadcrumbs
> 1/2 clove garlic, mashed
> 4 lamb backstrap fillets
> string

Cut eggplant into 1 cm slices and fry gently in olive oil until golden on both sides. Tip into a glass bowl and mash with a fork. Add the remaining ingredients, except lamb, and mash very well.

Split the lamb backstrap fillets along one side, keeping them in one piece, and open them out. Divide the stuffing into four and spread down the centre of each lamb fillet. Reform and tie with string.

Heat a little olive oil in a heavy-based, non-stick frying-pan and cook the lamb fillets for 4 minutes on each side. Remove and rest in a warm spot for 10 minutes. Serve with a fresh green salad.

☞ Hint: See Eggplants, To Salt or Not to Salt, page 7

Desserts

Italian bread pudding with pears

THE FIRM Beurre Bosc and Packham pears are my choice for this recipe as they hold their shape.

Serves 6

- 3 eggs
- $1/2$ cup castor sugar
- 1 teaspoon vanilla essence
- 1 cup cream
- 1 cup milk
- $1/2$ cup chopped dried pears, soaked in rum for at least 1 hour
- 1 pinch ground cinnamon
- zest of 1 lime, 1 lemon, 1 orange, chopped finely
- $1/2$ Italian panettone loaf, broken into 2 cm chunks or sliced
- extra sugar
- cream to serve

Baked vanilla pears

- 4 pears, peeled, cored and halved
- 1 cup white wine
- $1/3$ cup sugar
- 1 vanilla bean, split
- 1 cinnamon stick
- 30 g softened butter

Place the eggs, castor sugar, vanilla, cream and milk in a bowl and whisk well. Add the pears, cinnamon and zests and combine well.

Spread a layer of panettone over the base of a pudding bowl. Pour over some of the custard mixture and leave to soak in. Repeat until all ingredients are used. Sprinkle the top with extra sugar and bake in a 180°C oven for 20 minutes until the pudding is golden brown and shiny.

To prepare the baked vanilla pears: Place the pears in a baking dish and pour over white wine and sugar. Add the vanilla, cinnamon stick and dot with softened butter.

Bake in the oven with the pudding for about 1 hour, depending on the ripeness of the pears, then serve together.

☞ *Hint: See To Make Vanilla Sugar, page 17*

Chocolate banana pudding

NOT ONLY chocoholics will love this dessert, everyone will find it irresistible.

Serves 6–8

    125 g butter, softened
    1 cup castor sugar
    1 teaspoon vanilla essence
    2 eggs
    3 ripe bananas, mashed
    2 cups self-raising flour, sifted
    1 cup milk

Chocolate sauce

1/2 cup cocoa powder
3/4 cup brown sugar
2 1/2 cups boiling water
1 tablespoon butter

Preheat the oven to 180°C. Grease a large ovenproof dish.

Cream the butter, sugar and vanilla until light, then beat in the eggs, one at a time. Add the bananas and stir in the flour alternately with the milk. Pour mixture into greased dish.

To prepare sauce: Combine all ingredients and gently pour over pudding. Place in preheated oven and bake for 40–50 minutes.

Serve with whipped cream or ice-cream.

☞ *Hint: See Creaming Butter, page 5*

Raspberry sables

A CLASSICAL recipe with a dramatic presentation, guaranteed to please your dinner guests. You will need an 8 mm heart-shaped cutter for this recipe.

Serves 6

> **200 g unsalted butter, softened**
> **3/4 cup icing sugar, sifted**
> **2 egg yolks, lightly beaten**
> **2 cups flour, sifted**
> **grated rind of 1 lemon**
> **fresh raspberries**
> **whipped cream or heavy pure cream**
> **icing sugar for dusting**

Cream the butter and sugar in a bowl until light and fluffy. Add egg yolks gradually, beating well with each addition. Add flour and lemon rind and mix until just combined.

Wrap the shortbread in plastic wrap and refrigerate for several hours.

Roll out the shortbread to 2 mm thickness on a floured surface. Using an 8 mm heart-shaped cutter, cut 18 hearts and arrange on baking sheets.

Preheat the oven to 200°C and bake for 8–10 minutes or until just golden brown.

Allow to cool for 5 minutes before removing from the trays.

Sandwich the hearts together with raspberries and cream and dust with icing sugar before serving.

☞ *Hint: See Creaming Butter, page 5*

Buttermilk pancakes

FOR A Canadian-style breakfast, serve with crisp bacon, fried eggs, whipped butter and maple syrup.

Makes 8–10

- 1 cup plain flour
- 1 teaspoon baking powder
- 1/4 teaspoon salt
- 1/3 cup castor sugar
- 1 egg, lightly beaten
- 1 teaspoon vegetable oil
- 1 cup buttermilk (add 1/2 cup of extra milk if the buttermilk is thick) ☞
- 150 g butter, softened
- 2 tablespoons maple syrup

Sift together the flour, baking powder and salt. Add the remaining ingredients, except the butter and maple syrup, and mix until combined. It should be a thick but pourable batter.

Heat a griddle or very clean barbecue hot plate and brush with oil. Pour about 1/4 cup of batter onto the hot plate. Cook until bubbles appear. Turn over and cook the other side. Repeat with remaining mixture.

Beat the butter with electric beaters until pale and fluffy. Slowly beat in the maple syrup until well incorporated and very light. Serve over hot pancakes.

☞ Hint: See Buttermilk, page 4

Chocolate mousse

FOR THE best flavoured chocolate mousse, don't compromise on the quality of the chocolate—use a good eating chocolate.

Serves 6

   200 g dark eating chocolate
   2 tablespoons very strong coffee
   3 eggs, separated ☞
   15 g butter
   2 teaspoons dark rum or a few drops of vanilla essence
   pinch of cream of tartar

Break the chocolate into small pieces and place in a small saucepan with the coffee. Stir over gentle heat (or in microwave) until melted and smooth.

Add the yolks, one at a time, stirring well after each addition—the chocolate should be just hot enough to slightly cook the egg yolks. Remove from the heat and stir in the butter and rum.

In a clean bowl, whisk the eggwhites and cream of tartar to soft peaks and then whisk a little of the chocolate mixture quickly into the whites. Gently fold the remaining chocolate mixture into the eggwhites, taking care not to overmix, then pour into a serving bowl or glasses. Chill for about 2 hours or until set.

Serve with cream.

☞ *Hint: See Eggwhites, page 8*

Pumpkin tarts

USE AUSSIE pecans for this recipe—their flavour is great. However, pecans are not good storers so make sure you use only the freshest.

Sweet pastry

$^1/_2$ cup pecan nuts ☞
75 g salted butter
1 egg yolk
$^1/_4$ teaspoon vanilla essence
50 g icing sugar
125 g plain flour

Filling

500 g peeled and cubed butternut pumpkin
50 g butter
1 tablespoon brown sugar
$^1/_2$ cup castor sugar
3 teaspoons cornflour
1 teaspoon ground cinnamon
$^1/_2$ teaspoon ginger
3 eggs
$^1/_2$ cup cream
$^1/_2$ cup sour cream
a few pecan nuts for serving
icing sugar

Place the nuts, butter, yolk, vanilla, and icing sugar in the food processor and blend to a paste. Add the flour and pulse to mix in the flour.

Remove the pastry from the bowl and wrap in plastic wrap. Chill for about an hour before using, then use to line tartlet tins or a 20–23 cm tart tin or pie dish.

To prepare filling: Place the cubed pumpkin in a pan with the butter and the brown sugar and cook, tossing frequently, over low heat until the pumpkin is very soft. Set aside to cool.

Place the castor sugar, cornflour, cinnamon and ginger in a food processor. Add the cooled pumpkin and process until smooth. Add the eggs, cream and sour cream and process to combine. Pour the filling into the pie crust or tartlets and bake in a preheated 180°C oven for about 45 minutes or until the filling is set.

Place the pecan nuts on a piece of foil and dust with icing sugar. Melt the sugar under a hot griller. Serve the tarts with the nuts and some cream.

☞ *Hint: See To Store Nuts, page 11*

Chocolate rice pudding cake

IF YOU feel like varying the old favourite a little, here's an idea.

  1 1/2 cups short-grain rice
  4 cups milk
  1 teaspoon vanilla essence
  200 g butter
  1 cup castor sugar
  4 eggs, separated ☞
  1/2 cup self-raising flour
  1/2 cup cocoa powder
  icing sugar for dusting
  whipped cream for serving

Combine rice, milk and vanilla in a pan and simmer for 20 minutes, cool slightly. This step can also be done in the microwave.

Preheat the oven to 180°C. Grease a 23–25 cm cake tin and line the base with non-stick baking paper.

Beat the butter and half the sugar until light and fluffy. Add the egg yolks and beat until incorporated. Stir in the cooled rice and then the flour which has been sifted with the cocoa powder.

Beat the eggwhites with an electric beater until stiff, then beat in the remaining sugar. Fold through the rice mixture and spoon into the prepared tin. Level the surface and bake for 1 1/2 hours in the preheated oven. A skewer inserted in the cake may still be slightly sticky. Unmould and cool on a wire rack.

Dust with icing sugar and serve with whipped cream and stewed fruit.

☞ Hint: See Eggwhites, page 8

Chocolate souffle

WHO SAYS souffles are difficult? This is an easy, no-fail recipe.

Serves 4

2 cups milk
1 tablespoon butter
75 g cocoa powder, sifted
1/2 cup flour
1/2 cup cornflour
a little extra milk

To make the base recipe, bring the milk and butter to the boil in a saucepan and whisk in the sifted cocoa. Mix the flour and cornflour together and make a paste with milk. Whisk this mixture into the pan until you have a thick, heavy base.

Pour into a bowl, cool and cover with plastic wrap. This should keep in the fridge for up to a week.

To make the souffles, first butter and sugar small dishes.

Take about 1 cup of the base mixture and whisk with some brandy, rum or liqueur over heat until it is smooth but still quite thick.

Whisk about 4 eggwhites in a mixer until stiff peaks form. Add about 1/2 cup castor sugar (or to taste) and continue whisking until the sugar has dissolved.

Gently fold a little meringue into the base mixture and then the rest.

Fill the prepared moulds with the mixture and level off the top. Sprinkle with flaked almonds and bake in a preheated 200°C oven for about 12 15 minutes until the souffles are well risen and firm.

Serve straight away with cream and ice-cream.

☞ Hint: See Souffles, page 16

Figs in brandy syrup

LOTS OF style, no fuss—an ideal recipe, one that I'm often asked for.

Serves 2–4

> ¹/₂ cup brown sugar
> ¹/₂ cup brandy
> ¹/₂ cup apple juice
> 1 vanilla bean (or 1 teaspoon vanilla essence)
> 1 cinnamon stick
> 6 figs, halved
> cream or natural yoghurt to serve

Place brown sugar, brandy and apple juice in a saucepan. Stir to dissolve sugar. Bring to the boil and simmer for 5 minutes.

Add the vanilla bean and cinnamon stick and simmer for 2 minutes. Add figs and gently simmer for 3–4 minutes.

Serve with cream or yoghurt.

☞ *Hint: See To Make Vanilla Sugar, page 17*

Cakes & Biscuits

Rich fruit loaf

THIS RECIPE contains no added fat or added sugar—the almond meal is the main contributor to the small amount of fat in this recipe. It is also high in potassium thanks to the dried fruits.

Serves 10

200 g dried apricots
100 g dried figs
100 g dried prunes
100 g dried pears
2 cups water
1 cup wholemeal self-raising flour
1/2 cup almond meal
2 ripe bananas, mashed
1/2 teaspoon ground cinnamon
1/2 teaspoon mixed spice
1 teaspoon finely grated lemon rind

Place the dried fruits in a saucepan with water. Bring to the boil, cover and simmer for 5 minutes to soften the fruit. Purée fruit mixture and cooking liquid.

Preheat the oven to 180°C. Grease and line a 20 cm loaf tin.

Mix the flour and almond meal in a large bowl. Add fruit purée, bananas, cinnamon, mixed spice and lemon rind.

Pour mixture into a greased loaf tin and bake in the oven for 40 minutes or until a skewer inserted into the centre comes out clean.

Allow to cool before turning out onto a rack.

☞ *Hint: See Cakes, pages 4*

Orange semolina cake

I LOVE syrup-soaked cakes. This one is sticky, tangy and very moist.

250 g butter
1 cup castor sugar
2 tablespoons grated orange rind
4 eggs
3 tablespoons brandy
2 cups semolina
2 1/2 cups ground almonds
2 teaspoons baking powder

Syrup

1 cup sugar
2 1/2 cups orange juice

Preheat the oven to 200°C. Cream the butter, sugar and orange rind until light and fluffy. Beat in the eggs one at a time, then stir in the brandy.

Combine semolina, almonds and baking powder and fold lightly into creamed mixture. Turn into a greased 24 cm springform tin.

Place in the oven and immediately lower the heat to 180°C. Bake until firm, about 45 minutes to 1 hour.

To prepare the syrup: Combine the sugar and orange juice in a small saucepan. Stir until sugar dissolves before bringing to the boil. Boil for 5 minutes. Cool slightly. Remove the cake from oven and pour over the syrup while in the tin.

☞ *Hint: See Creaming Butter, page 5*

Apple and date roll

IF YOU can make scones, this roll is just as easy. Granny Smith apples are a good choice for this recipe.

1 cup self-raising flour, sifted
1/2 cup plain flour, sifted
pinch of salt
80 g butter
1/4 cup milk
1/4 cup water
1/3 cup brown sugar
2 teaspoons ground cinnamon
1/4 teaspoon ground cloves
1 green apple, peeled and grated ☞
1/2 cup chopped dates

Butterscotch sauce

125 g butter
1 cup brown sugar
1 tablespoon lemon juice
1/4 cup water

Preheat the oven to 190°C.

Place the flours and salt into a large bowl. Rub 50 g of the butter into the flour mixture until it resembles coarse breadcrumbs. Stir in the milk and water and mix to form a soft dough.

Knead lightly on a floured surface, then roll out to form a 20 x 25 cm rectangle.

Melt the remaining butter and brush a little over the dough. Sprinkle with brown sugar, cinnamon and cloves. Spread the apple and dates over the dough, then roll up like a Swiss roll.

Place in a greased baking tin and bake for 10 minutes, then pour over the butterscotch sauce. Bake for a further 20–25 minutes, then serve with cream or ice-cream.

To prepare the butterscotch sauce: Simmer all ingredients together for 2 minutes, then pour over the roll.

☞ *Hint: See Apples For Cooking, page 2*

Triple chocolate chiffon cake

A GOOD investment is an Angel Food cake tin (also known as a high tube tin). They are available in specialty kitchen stores, so why not get yourself one and try this lovely, light cake.

1 ¼ cups plain flour
½ cup cornflour
3 teaspoons baking powder
1 teaspoon salt
1 ¾ cups sugar
½ cup cocoa powder
¾ cup boiling water
½ cup vegetable oil
7 egg yolks
1 teaspoon vanilla essence
100 g grated chocolate
7 eggwhites ☞
½ teaspoon cream of tartar

Chocolate glaze

90 g dark chocolate, chopped
60 g unsalted butter
2 teaspoons corn syrup

Preheat the oven to 160°C. Sift together the flour, cornflour, baking powder, salt and sugar. Mix the cocoa and boiling water until smooth and set aside to cool. Add the oil, egg yolks, cocoa mixture and vanilla to the flour mixture and mix well to combine. Stir in the grated chocolate.

In a large clean bowl, whisk the eggwhites with the cream of tartar until very stiff peaks form. Pour the egg yolk mixture gradually over the whipped whites, gently folding in with a rubber scraper until just blended. Pour into an ungreased Angel Food tin and bake in the preheated oven.

When the cake is cooked, cool inverted in the tin. Unmould and ice with chocolate glaze.

To prepare the chocolate glaze: Place the chocolate, butter and corn syrup in a microwave-safe bowl and microwave on MEDIUM for 20 seconds. Check, stir and heat in 20 second bursts until the mixture is smooth. Or place chocolate, butter and corn syrup in a heatproof bowl over simmering water and heat, stirring, until chocolate is melted and well combined. Pour the glaze over cake.

☞ *Hint: See Overbeating Eggwhites, page 8*

Plum baked cheesecake

PLUMS ARE a wonderful fruit for desserts—their rich, deep colour adds to the presentation and in this recipe, their acid cuts through the richness of the cheese to create a delicious balance.

75 g butter, melted
75 g unblanched almonds, roasted
75 g sweet biscuit crumbs
500 g ripe blood plums, halved and pitted
250 g cream cheese
1/3 cup sour cream
50 g castor sugar
1 teaspoon vanilla essence
75 ml milk, heated
2 tablespoons cornflour
4 eggs, separated ☞
80 g castor sugar, extra

Preheat the oven to 210°C. Combine the melted butter, almonds and biscuit crumbs in a bowl and mix well. Press into the base of a 20 cm springform cake tin. Arrange the plums, cut-side down, over the base.

Place the cream cheese, sour cream, castor sugar and vanilla in the bowl of an electric mixer and cream until smooth. Add the hot milk and beat until smooth, then add the cornflour and yolks.

In a clean bowl, whisk the eggwhites until firm peaks form, then whisk in the extra sugar to make a firm meringue. Fold the meringue into the cheese mixture and pour over the plum base.

Bake in the oven for 15 minutes, then reduce the temperature to 160°C and bake for a further 20 minutes or until a skewer inserted into the cake comes out clean. Serve cold, dusted with icing sugar.

☞ Hint: See Eggwhites, page 8

Easy chocolate cake

EMERGENCY! I need a delicious cake fast! Well, here it is.

200 g dark eating chocolate ☞
125 g butter
²/₃ cup self-raising flour
²/₃ cup castor sugar
4 eggs
cream for serving
icing sugar for dusting

Preheat the oven to 175°C.

Melt the chocolate and butter together in the microwave or over boiling water.

Allow to cool a little, then add the flour, sugar and eggs. Beat well for 3 minutes, then pour the mixture into a greased 20 cm springform tin.

Bake for 30–35 minutes or until the centre is still quite moist when tested with a skewer.

Cool in the tin for 10 minutes before turning out onto a wire rack. Serve with cream, dusted with icing sugar.

☞ *Hint: See To Melt Chocolate, page 6*

American-style strawberry shortcake

ONLY THE best strawberries will do for this recipe, any less won't be worth your while. When choosing a punnet, check to make sure that there are no fluids at the bottom—this will tell you whether or not they have been sitting around too long.

    1 cup plain flour
    1 cup self-raising flour
    1/3 cup castor sugar
    25 g butter, chilled
    1/4 cup cream
    1/4–1/2 cup milk
    1 egg
    2 punnets strawberries, washed and hulled ☞
    1/4 cup sugar, extra
    liqueur of choice such as framboise (optional)
    1 1/2 cups cream, extra, lightly whipped
    icing sugar for dusting

Preheat the oven to 220°C.

Sift the flours and castor sugar into a bowl and add the cold butter. Rub in with your fingertips until the mixture resembles coarse breadcrumbs. Pour the cream, milk and egg into a well in the flour mixture and cut through with a knife until it just amalgamates. Add more milk if needed to form a very soft dough. Press the mixture into a greased 20 cm cake tin and bake in the oven for 25–30 minutes, or until a skewer inserted into the centre of the cake comes out clean.

While the shortcake is baking, halve the strawberries and toss in the sugar. Add a little liqueur if you wish. Allow the strawberries to stand for at least 30 minutes.

To assemble the cake, turn the shortcake out of the tin and split into 2 layers.

Spoon half the whipped cream onto the bottom layer and top with half the strawberries. Place the second layer of shortcake, cut-side down on top of the strawberries and cream. Top with remaining cream and strawberries.

Dust with icing sugar and serve warm.

☞ *Hint: See To Wash Strawberries, page 16*

Texas sheet cake

THIS IS a very popular recipe sent in by a 'What's Cooking' viewer—
y'all should try it.

2 cups plain flour
2 teaspoons baking powder
2 cups castor sugar
125 g salted butter
3 tablespoons cocoa powder
1 cup water
1/2 cup buttermilk
2 eggs, lightly beaten
1 teaspoon salt
1 teaspoon ground cinnamon
1 teaspoon vanilla essence

Icing

1/2 cup unsalted butter
4 tablespoons cocoa powder
6 tablespoons milk
3 1/2 cups icing sugar
1 teaspoon vanilla essence
1 cup chopped pecan nuts

Preheat the oven to 180°C.

Sift the flour and baking powder into a large mixing bowl, mix in the
sugar and set aside.

Combine the butter, cocoa and water in a saucepan and slowly bring
to the boil. Pour the cocoa mixture over the flour mixture and mix
well. Stir in the buttermilk, eggs, salt, cinnamon and vanilla.

Pour into a greased and floured lamington pan and bake in the oven
for 35 minutes or until firm.

To prepare the icing: Begin making the icing 5 minutes before the cake is done. Allow the cake to cool for 5 minutes and ice while it is still warm. In a medium-size saucepan, combine the butter, cocoa and milk and slowly bring to the boil. Remove from the heat and add the icing sugar, mixing well. Stir in the vanilla and nuts.

Pour the icing sugar over the cake and enjoy warm or cold.

☞ *Hint: See Cakes, page 4*

Hummingbird cake

ANOTHER POPULAR favourite from our American cousins.

- 3 cups flour
- 1 teaspoon bicarbonate of soda
- 2 cups castor sugar
- 1 teaspoon ground cinnamon
- 3/4 cup pecans or walnuts, roughly chopped
- 1 cup canola oil
- 3 eggs
- 425 g can crushed pineapple
- 4–6 ripe bananas, mashed
- 1 teaspoon vanilla essence

Cream cheese icing

- 100 g butter, softened
- 375 g cream cheese, softened
- 1 teaspoon vanilla essence
- 2 teaspoons lemon juice
- 3/4 cup icing sugar

Sift the dry ingredients together into a mixing bowl. Mix the oil and eggs together and add to the dry ingredients. Stir until mixed but do not beat. Mix in the undrained pineapple, banana and vanilla.

Divide between two, greased 23 cm round cake tins and bake in a 180°C oven for 50 minutes or until a skewer inserted in the centre of the cake comes out clean.

Allow to stand for 5 minutes, then turn out onto a wire rack. Cool completely, cut into 2 rounds, then sandwich together with cream cheese icing.

To prepare the cream cheese icing: Mash the butter and cream cheese together. Add the remaining ingredients and mix well. Do not overbeat as the mixture will become too runny.

Honey and almond cake

THIS IS a great cake to make for your next afternoon tea.

3 eggs
125 g castor sugar
few drops of vanilla essence
75 g butter, melted
2 tablespoons pure cream
150 g plain flour
$^1/_2$ teaspoon baking powder

Topping

100 g butter
80 g castor sugar
75 g thick honey ☞
2 tablespoons double cream
150 g flaked almonds
$^1/_2$ teaspoon ground cinnamon
grated rind of $^1/_2$ an orange

Preheat the oven to 200°C. Grease a 25 cm springform tin.

Whisk the eggs with the sugar and vanilla until frothy. Stir in the cooled butter and cream. Sift the flour and baking powder into the mixture and fold in. Pour into the prepared tin and bake for about 15 minutes or until a crust has set on the top.

To prepare the topping: Melt the butter in a pan and add the sugar, honey, cream, almonds, cinnamon and orange rind. Stir the ingredients well and bring them to the boil. Spread this mixture over the cake and return to the oven for a further 15–20 minutes.

Loosen the cake from the tin and leave to cool on a wire rack.

☞ *Hint: See To Handle Honey More Easily, page 9*

Scottish oatcakes

THESE MELT-in-the-mouth oatmeal biscuits are traditionally served with cheese but they are equally delicious spread with butter, jam or honey. Handle with care, they are inclined to be brittle.

> 300 g fine or medium oatmeal
> 1/2 teaspoon salt
> 150 ml hot water (approx.)
> 1–2 tablespoons melted butter or oil

Preheat the oven to 160°C.

Mix oatmeal and salt in a medium-size mixing bowl. Make a well in the centre and pour in the hot water and butter. Mix to a stiff paste (this can also be done in a food processor). Turn onto a floured surface and roll out as quickly as possible so that the mixture does not dry out.

Using a saucepan lid or saucer, cut out large rounds and cut into farls (3 cornered pieces). Slide onto a baking tray and bake in the preheated oven for about 10 minutes (the edges will curl slightly). Cool, then store in an airtight container.

☞ *Hint: See Rolling Biscuit Dough, page 2*

Chocolate almond bread

THESE ARE elegant little companions to a cup of tea or coffee. Once baked and dried out they are extremely fragile so handle with care.

6 eggwhites ☞
a pinch of cream of tartar
100 g castor sugar
180 g plain flour, sifted
20 g cocoa powder, sifted
250 g unblanched almonds or hazelnuts
80 g dark chocolate, grated

Preheat the oven to 170°C

In a very clean bowl, whisk the eggwhites and cream of tartar until soft peaks form. Add the sugar and continue beating until firm and glossy.

Fold in the sifted flour and cocoa, the whole nuts and chocolate and spoon into a greased loaf tin.

Bake in the preheated oven for about 40–50 minutes or until a skewer inserted in the centre of the loaf comes out clean.

Turn the loaf out of its tin, wrap in a clean tea-towel and store in a plastic bag overnight. Leave for 24 hours before cutting (the loaf can be frozen at this stage).

Slice the almond bread thinly with a sharp serrated knife and lay the slices out on the oven shelves or a baking tray.

Bake in a 160°C oven until dry and the almonds lightly browned. Store in an airtight container.

☞ *Hint: See Eggwhites, page 8*

Breads

Focaccia bread

ONE OF the most popular and versatile breads these days. Here's how to make your own at home.

Makes 1

1 tablespoon dried yeast (or 2 tablespoons fresh)
6 cups unbleached bread flour
2 1/2 cups warm water
1 tablespoon ground rock-salt
1 tablespoon fresh rosemary leaves
3 tablespoons olive oil
sea-salt

Mix the yeast with the flour and add the warm water, rock-salt, rosemary and olive oil and mix well. When the dough is beginning to come together, turn out onto a floured surface and start to knead.

Continue kneading until the dough is silky and smooth, about 10 minutes. Place the dough in a well-oiled bowl and allow to rise until doubled in size.

Turn the dough out and divide into two or four equal portions. With your fingertips, gently stretch the dough to the shape you require. Traditionally, the focaccia bread should be oval shaped, but it can be any shape you please. At this point you can flavour the focaccia with any topping you desire.

Cover the dough with a damp tea-towel and allow to rise until doubled, about 1 hour. With your fingertips, vigorously dimple the dough all over, making sure that the holes are quite deep. Set aside to rise again for a further hour.

Gently brush with extra oil and sprinkle with sea-salt. Bake the focaccia bread, on a baking stone if you have one, in a 200°C oven for 20–25 minutes. During the cooking time, remember to spray the focaccia bread with water. This will improve the moisture content of the bread and give a crispy crust.

Variations

Herb focaccia: Add 1/2 cup chopped fresh herbs, such as basil, dill, parsley and chives to the dough when first mixing and process as above.

Rosemary/sage focaccia: When the dough has been shaped, sprinkle the top with finely chopped rosemary or sage leaves when brushing with oil.

Olive focaccia: Add 1 cup pitted, chopped olives to the dough when first mixing and continue as above or sprinkle the chopped olives on top of the dough after shaping and before baking. A combination of black and green olives looks lovely.

Caramelised onion focaccia: Peel two large onions and sweat in 2 tablespoons olive oil. Turn the heat down to the lowest setting and cook, covered, for about 40 minutes or until the onions are golden brown.

Savoury croissants: Roll the focaccia dough out to a rectangle about 1 cm thick. Spread with your chosen toppings and then cut the dough into triangles. Roll each triangle up from the base, toward the point to form the croissant shape. Allow to rise for 30 minutes, then bake in a 220°C oven for 12 minutes or until golden.

Some of my favourite toppings are: pesto, tapenade, sun-dried tomato paste, olives, cheese, diced capsicum, cold diced meats, mushrooms and fresh herbs.

Hot cross buns

JUST LIKE Christmas puddings, there's something particularly rewarding about baking your own Hot Cross Buns. I guess it's because you could and should involve the kids.

Makes 16

30 g fresh yeast or 2 sachets of dried yeast ☞
pinch sugar
$1/2$ cup lukewarm water
500 g plain flour
2 tablespoons gluten flour
$1/2$ teaspoon salt
1 teaspoon ground cinnamon
50 g soft butter
4 tablespoons brown sugar
$1/2$ cup boiled milk, cooled
1 egg
$1/2$ cup chopped dried apricots
$1/2$ cup chopped dried dates or figs
$1/2$ cup chopped pecans or walnuts

Crosses

4 $1/2$ tablespoons flour
3 tablespoons water
1 teaspoon vegetable oil

Bun glaze

$1/4$ cup sugar
$1/4$ cup water
1 teaspoon gelatine
$1/4$ teaspoon ground cinnamon

Preheat the oven to 220°C.

Mix yeast with a pinch of sugar and a little of the water and allow to ferment for about 15 minutes.

Sift the flours, salt and cinnamon together. Rub in the butter, using your fingertips, then stir in the sugar.

Make a well in the centre of the flour mixture, pour in the yeast mixture, remaining water, milk and egg. Mix to form a soft dough, adding a little extra water if necessary.

Turn onto a lightly floured surface and knead until smooth and elastic, about 5 minutes. Press out into a flat shape and add the fruit and nuts. Roll up and knead a little more until the fruit is well distributed through the dough. Place in a lightly-oiled bowl, cover and allow to stand in a warm place until double in size, about 40 minutes. Turn out onto a lightly floured surface and punch down. Cut into 16 pieces and knead each piece into a round. Place on a greased baking tray about 1 cm apart to allow for spreading. Cover and stand in a warm place until well risen, about 15 minutes.

To prepare crosses: Combine the cross ingredients to form a smooth paste. Pour into a freezer bag, tie the top and cut off one corner to form a 3 mm opening. Pipe this mixture to form crosses on the buns. Bake buns in the preheated oven for about 20 minutes.

Place buns on a wire cooling rack and brush with glaze.

To prepare bun glaze: Combine all ingredients in a small saucepan. Stir over low heat until sugar is dissolved. Bring to the boil. Brush over buns while hot.

🖙 *Hint: See Fresh Yeast, page 3*

Filled country loaf

THIS LOAF is just perfect for a picnic.

Serves 4–6

> 1 small sesame or poppy seed topped cob loaf or
>   pasta dura loaf
> 1 clove garlic, cut in half
> 2 sweet red capsicums, seeded, cored and cut into
>   thick strips
> olive oil
> 2 eggplant, sliced ☞
> 2 vine-ripened tomatoes, sliced
> freshly ground black pepper to taste
> 1/2 bunch fresh basil leaves
> 200 g thinly sliced mortadella

Cut the top from the loaf and pull out the bread from the inside (the bread can be used for breadcrumbs). Rub with a cut garlic clove and brush lightly with olive oil.

Toss the capsicum strips in olive oil and place them skin-side up on the griller tray. Grill until the skin blisters and begins to blacken. Turn over and cook the other side.

While the capsicum is cooking, brush the eggplant slices lightly with olive oil. When the capsicum is done, remove them and grill the eggplant slices until they are nice and brown. Cool and skin the capsicum.

Place a layer of eggplant slices in the base of the bread shell. Top with a layer of capsicum and tomatoes, black pepper, basil and plenty of mortadella. Repeat layers until everything is used up. Replace lid, press down firmly, wrap tightly in a clean tea-towel and refrigerate for at least 12 hours to allow the flavours to develop.
Cut into wedges and serve.

☞ Hint: See Eggplant, page 7

Cheese and basil scones

DELICIOUS SPREAD with butter straight from the oven, or serve them with soup such as Roasted Tomato.

Makes about 12

1 tablespoon butter
2 cups self-raising flour
1/3 cup grated Cheddar cheese
1/4 teaspoon salt
1/3 cup chopped fresh basil
freshly ground black pepper to taste
3/4–1 cup milk

Preheat the oven to 220°C. Rub the butter into the flour until the mixture resembles breadcrumbs. Add the cheese, salt, basil and pepper.

Carefully mix through the milk using a knife blade to form a dough.

Press out by hand to a thickness of 15 mm and cut into rounds. Arrange on a greased baking tray and bake in the hot oven for about 10 minutes.

☞ *Hint: See Baking Scones, page 5*

Beer bread

THIS RECIPE is inspired by Paul Mercurio and his friends at the Lord Nelson Hotel in Sydney. Who said bread making can't be easy?

600 ml dark ale
80 g butter, melted
1/2 cup golden syrup, warmed
1 egg
pinch of salt
self-raising flour

Preheat the oven to 150°C.

Whisk the beer, butter, golden syrup and egg together and add flour until the mixture no longer sticks to the hands. Cover and let stand overnight.

Pour onto a floured tray and shape into a round loaf.

Slash the top with a sharp knife and bake in the preheated oven for 1 hour 20 minutes.

☞ *Hint: See Bread, page 3*

Cornbread

AN AMERICAN favourite, cornbread goes well with cajun-style recipes.

1 3/4 cups yellow cornmeal ☞
1 cup plain flour
1 tablespoon baking powder
1/4 cup sugar
2 eggs, beaten
185 g butter, melted
1 1/4 cups milk

Preheat the oven to 200°C.

Sift cornmeal, flour and baking powder into a bowl and add sugar. Mix eggs with melted butter and milk. Pour into dry ingredients and beat well. Pour into a greased and lined square tin and bake in the preheated oven for 45 minutes. Cool and cut into 10 cm squares.

☞ Hint: See Buying and Storing Cornmeal, page 6

Choux pastry

CHOUX PASTRY can be used for a number of savoury, as well as sweet, dishes and adds an impressive touch to the simplest of meals. Choux paste can also be simply deep-fried or baked and piped with a sweet or savoury filling when cold.

> 1 cup water
> 125 g butter, cut into pieces
> 175 g plain flour, sifted
> 4–5 eggs (60 g) at room temperature

Bring the water and butter to the boil, stirring from time to time. Remove from the heat. Add the sifted flour all at once.

Using a wooden spatula, slowly work the flour and liquid together. Stir vigorously, until the ball of paste sticks neither to the pan nor the spatula.

Add the eggs one at a time, beating well after each addition. (This can be done by machine.)

Check the consistency of the batter; a peak should just fall back on itself.

Variations

Gougere ring: Mix 60 g grated Gruyere (or other Swiss-style cheese) through 2 cups choux paste, then drop spoonfuls around the inside of a greased springform tin. Sprinkle with 60 g extra grated cheese.

Bake in a 200°C oven for 40–45 minutes until puffed and golden. Do not open the oven door during baking. Serve straight from the oven.

Potatoes dauphine: Mix two parts mashed potato with 1 part choux paste. Drop spoonfuls into hot oil and deep-fry until puffed and golden.

Parisienne gnocchi: Mix equal parts of choux paste and mashed potato. Drop teaspoonfuls of paste into boiling water and simmer until the gnocchi float to the surface. Serve with your choice of sauce.

Edible salad bowl: Spread a thin layer of choux paste over a large piece of non-stick paper, then drape it over a stainless steel bowl or cake tin.

Bake in a 210°C oven, reducing the temperature to 180°C after about 15 minutes. Bake until the pastry is quite dry and brown.

This can be made ahead and stored in an airtight container.

Sticky apricot pecan scrolls

NO, YOU don't need to spend hours twisting dough into scrolls—just roll it up like a Swiss roll, slice and bake.

Dough

2 cups plain flour
pinch of salt
1 teaspoon ground cardamom
1 1/2 cups pouring cream

Filling

250 g dried apricots
1 cup water
100 g butter
1/2 cup brown sugar
1 tablespoon lemon juice
1/2 cup roughly chopped pecan nuts ☞

Syrup

1/4 cup sugar
1/4 cup water
1 tablespoon honey
1 tablespoon lemon juice
1 teaspoon ground cardamom

To prepare the filling: Place the apricots in a microwave-safe bowl with the water and microwave on HIGH for about 5 minutes or until soft (alternatively, simmer in a saucepan for 10 minutes on the stove). Allow to cool.

Place the butter and brown sugar in a food processor and blend until creamy. Add the cooled apricots with their liquid and the lemon juice and process to combine. Stir the nuts through by hand.

To prepare the dough: Sift the flour, salt and cardamom into a mixing bowl and mix through the cream with the blade of a knife.

Turn out onto a floured surface and knead very lightly. Press or roll out to form a 30 x 30 cm square.

Spread with the filling and roll up like a Swiss roll. Cut into 3 cm thick slices and arrange in a greased springform cake tin.

Bake in a 200°C oven for about 30 minutes or until golden brown.

To prepare the syrup: Simmer the syrup ingredients together for 2 minutes.

Remove the scrolls from the oven and pour over the hot syrup. Serve warm.

☞ *Hint: See To Store Nuts, page 11*

Basics

Basic coulis recipe

You can use this recipe for strawberries, raspberries, or whatever berries are in season.

Makes 1 1/2 cups

> 1 punnet berries
> 1/2 cup sugar
> 1/2 cup water
> juice of 1/2 lemon

Boil the sugar and water together for a few minutes, then cool.

Place in a blender or food processor with the strawberries and lemon juice and purée. Strain and serve with a dessert. Use within a day or two.

Tomato sauce

Makes enough sauce for pasta for 4

> 1 medium-size onion, chopped
> 2 tablespoons olive oil
> 1 medium-size tomato, peeled and chopped
> 2 tablespoons tomato paste
> 1 1/2 cups water
> salt and freshly ground black pepper to taste

To prepare the tomato sauce: Sauté the onion in olive oil in a pan. Add the chopped tomato, paste and water. Season with salt and pepper and simmer until reduced to a sauce consistency.

Mayonnaise

2 egg yolks
1 ¹/₂ tablespoons red or white vinegar
salt and white pepper to taste
1–2 tablespoons Dijon mustard
1 ¹/₂ cups light olive oil

Drop the egg yolks into a bowl and using a whisk or electric beater, mix in the vinegar, salt, pepper and mustard.

Beating continuously, add the oil in a thin stream (very slowly at first or it may curdle). If you wish, you can beat in some boiling water to reach the desired consistency.

Home-made pasta

Pasta rolling machines make home-made pasta easy—just make the dough and roll it through. Start on the lowest setting and increase the setting as the pasta gets thinner. Once you have your sheets of pasta, you can cut them into any shape you desire.

Serves 4–6

400 g flour
pinch of salt
4 large eggs

Sift the flour and salt into a bowl. Make a well in the centre and break in the eggs. Work the flour into the eggs with a fork and continue with your hands until the ingredients are well mixed, adding a tablespoon or more of flour if necessary, so that the mass holds together well. Knead for 10–15 minutes until the dough is smooth and elastic, adding a little more flour if it is too sticky. Wrap in plastic wrap and leave to rest for 10–15 minutes at room temperature before rolling out.

For hand rolling: Divide the dough into 2 balls. Roll each out as thinly as possible on a lightly-floured surface with a lightly-floured rolling pin, working from the centre outwards. With experience you should be able to roll it out evenly, almost paper thin, without breaking it. Leave to dry for 20 minutes before cutting.

Pasta should be cooked until 'al dente', which means that there should be a little resistance in the pasta when you bite it. This way the texture is maintained and it is not mushy.

Rice

Absorption method

With this method, the rice cooks on the outside, and then when the steaming is taking place, moisture penetrates gently, gelatinising the centres. The lid must be kept firmly on during the entire cooking period—you must resist the temptation to lift the lid and see what is going on inside the pan.

For 500 g of rice use 4 cups of water. Put the rice and water into a large saucepan and bring to the boil. As soon as it comes to the boil, turn the heat very low, cover tightly with the saucepan lid and allow to cook for 20 minutes. The liquid should be completely absorbed and the rice cooked. Uncover and allow the steam to escape for a few minutes. Fluff the rice with a fork and serve with a metal spoon as a wooden spoon will crush the grains.

Alternatively, allow half a cup of rice per person, and wash the rice well in a sieve under running water. Shake out as much water as possible and put the rice in a heavy-based saucepan. Add 4 cups of cold water for each 3 cups of rice. Put on a low heat and allow to come to the boil, then cook, covered (with the heat as low as possible), until all the water is absorbed. This takes around 20 minutes.

> If you are cooking short-grain rice, remember that the absorption rate is not as great as that of long-grain rice. For 500 g of rice allow 2 1/2 cups of water for a very firm result, or 3 cups for a softer result.

> When steaming rice, the lid should not be lifted during cooking time as steam is lost and this affects the cooking time and the final result. Don't stir during the cooking.

> If you wash the rice, allow to drain thoroughly before cooking otherwise the measurements of water will not be accurate.

Trouble shooting—the burnt bottom: this can be a problem with the absorption method, but putting the hot pan onto a wet cloth when you take it off the stove can help unstick the grains from the bottom.

Rapid boil method

Wash the rice as above, then place in a large saucepan of boiling water. Keep it boiling vigorously until the rice is cooked, about 5 minutes. Strain the rice and immediately wash with cold running water to stop the cooking process. To warm the rice again, rinse with boiling water.

> Use a wide-based colander to drain the rice—if it is narrow and deep the rice will pack down and stick.

Trouble shooting: Some problems with the rapid boil method are that the rice gets knocked around during cooking and the grains can fray and split. It can be too soft on the outside and soggy in the centre. When it is cooked, you need to rinse it to get rid of the starch in the water, otherwise the rice turns into gum—it needs to cool down and tighten up.

For brown rice

Absorption method: Follow the absorption method using 2 cups water to 1 cup rice. Simmer for 55 minutes. For a firmer result, wash the rice and let soak in cooking water for at least 1 hour in the pan before bringing it to the boil and following the absorption method.

Rapid boil method: Use the rapid boil method but boil for 30–40 minutes, checking after 30 minutes.

Steamed rice

Place 1 cup of rice in a colander. Rinse under cold water, until the water runs clear. Allow the rice to drain and dry. Place in a heavy-based saucepan with enough water to cover by 25 mm. Bring to boil and boil rapidly until steam holes appear on the rice surface. Quickly reduce the heat to the lowest point and cover with a lid and simmer for 10 minutes. Uncover and fork lightly. Allow to stand for 5 minutes before serving to allow to firm up and settle down.

Shortcrust pastry

250 g plain flour
125 g unsalted butter
iced water

Process the flour and butter in a food processor until the mixture resembles coarse breadcrumbs. If making by hand, rub butter in with fingertips or cut in with two knives.

Add iced water while processor motor is running until dough holds together. If making by hand, mix with a knife or wooden spoon.

Press dough into a ball and wrap in plastic wrap and refrigerate for at least 30 minutes before rolling or shaping. Pastry can be stored in the fridge for several days or the freezer for up to 3 months.

To make sweet shortcrust pastry: Process 2 tablespoons castor sugar with the flour and butter.

☞ *Hint: See Resting Pastry, page 13*

Index of Recipes

Soups

Salads

Quick Meals & Snacks

Pasta & Rice

Seafood

Poultry

chicken 88
Creamy cajun-spiced chicken 85
Moroccan chicken couscous 82
Peking duck pancakes 94

Meat

Balti-style lamb chops with fragrant rice 106
Barbecued pork with peach salsa & zucchini couscous 102
Beef and bean red curry 103
Beef and sauerkraut hot pot 104
Braised lamb shanks with mushrooms and madeira 108
Crumbed lamb cutlets with garlic potato purée 110
Eggplant stuffed fillets of lamb 112
Rolled pork with spinach and chestnut stuffing 100
Thai pork curry with eggplant 98

Desserts

Buttermilk pancakes 118
Chocolate banana pudding 116
Chocolate mousse 119
Chocolate rice pudding cake 122
Chocolate souffle 123
Figs in brandy syrup 124
Italian bread pudding with pears 114
Pumpkin tarts 120
Raspberry sables 117

Cakes & Biscuits

American-style strawberry shortcake 134
Apple and date roll 128
Chocolate almond bread 141

Easy chocolate cake 133
Honey and almond cake 139
Hummingbird cake 138
Orange semolina cake 127
Plum baked cheesecake 132
Rich fruit loaf 126
Scottish oatcakes 140
Texas sheet cake 136
Triple chocolate chiffon cake 130

Breads

Beer bread 150
Cheese and basil scones 149
Choux pastry 152
Corn bread 151
Filled country loaf 148
Focaccia 144
Hot cross buns 146
Sticky apricot pecan scrolls 154

Basics

Coulis 156
Home-made pasta 157
Mayonnaise 157
Rice 158
Shortcrust pastry 160
Sweet shortcrust pastry 160
Tomato sauce 156

Join the Club!
The Geoff Jansz Recipe Club

Do you enjoy sharing recipes?
Want to find out more about great produce and the best suppliers?
Looking for answers to your culinary questions?
How about having access to an amazing range of seeds and how to grow them?
Do you want to be informed of the wonderful developments in Australian food as they happen?

Write to the address below and we will send you our monthly newsletter, commencing early 1996.

Recipe Club
PO Box 281
Bowral NSW 2576

If you want to begin sharing recipes or information with the club straightaway, we would be glad to receive your contributions—one or two recipes may even be featured on 'What's Cooking'.

Who's cooking with EUROLEC

$100 Cash Back on Your Eurolec Appliance Purchase

Purchaser's Name _____

Address _____

_____ P/code _____

Appliance _____

Salesperson's Signature _____ Date _____

Dealer _____ Invoice No. _____

Phone 1800 652 664 for Your Nearest Eurolec Dealer